THE FUTURE OF THE AMERICAN ECONOMY 2050

Miguel Peñaloza   Tomas Peñaloza

We dedicate this book to our families.

"We grow in different directions, yet our roots remain as one."

Suzy Kassem

"Nothing should be more obvious than that the business organism cannot function according to design when its most important 'parameters of action'—wages, prices, interest—are transferred to the political sphere and there dealt with according to the requirements of the political game or, which sometimes is more serious still, according to the ideas of some planners."

Joseph A. Schumpeter

ACKNOWLEDGEMENTS

The authors wish to express their gratitude to Holly Wallace for her valuable comments and suggestions. However, the authors assume full responsibility for any imperfections or shortcomings in the text.

TABLE OF CONTENTS

1. Introduction

2. Key Features of the American Economy

3. Economic Growth 1970 - 2022

4. Present and Future Growth Challenges

    A. Present Growth-Income Challenges
    B. Future Growth-Demographic Challenges
    C. Financial Challenges

5. Roadmap for Stronger Economic Growth

    A. Demand Side Recommendations
    B. Supply Side Recommendation

6. Financial Challenges and Needed Reforms

    A. Addressing Public Sector Challenges
    B. Addressing Private Sector Challenges

7. Epilogue

Technical Appendixes

Glossary

References

CHAPTER 1

INTRODUCTION

This book is about the Future (2050) of the American Economy. It is written for the public in general.

The purpose of this book is to show that while the American Economy continues to be the biggest economy in the world with outstanding features, both the worlds and the US's economies are encountering important challenges that could reduce their future economic growth. As it stands today, the US runs the risk, in the medium and long terms, of arriving at a state of stagnation or depression, like the one that occurred in the 1930s, if these issues are not addressed appropriately.

In our book "*ECONOMIC DECELERATION*", we explain why the American economy's growth has been slowing down for the past 50 years.

In this book we analyze the main challenges that continue to impact current and future potential economic growth of the American economy and we present a roadmap with recommendations that will provide the necessary solutions.

In our research we found out that not only quantitative solutions were necessary, but qualitative ones also. Therefore, in addressing these issues, we take into consideration the impact of the recommendations on the nation's economic development, because economic growth means an increase in real national income / national output, while economic development means an improvement in the quality of life and living standards, e.g. measures of literacy, life-expectancy, and health care.

Ceteris paribus, we would expect economic growth to enable more economic development since higher real Gross Domestic Product (GDP) enables more to be spent on health care and education. However, the link is not guaranteed. Therefore, the recommendations we make seek to have a favorable impact on most of the population.

In the first part of this book, we discuss the key features of the American economy.

We then proceed to summarize the key components that started the slowing down of the economy 50 years ago (most of the discussion comes from our previous publication "Economic Deceleration").

Next, we discuss present and future growth challenges, dividing these into current income challenges, future demographic challenges, and potential financial challenges.

We conclude with a roadmap for the American economy that will bring stronger economic growth, as well as economic development.

The roadmap includes recommendations that will impact aggregate demand, aggregate supply, and required financial reforms. The roadmap includes the public as well as the private sector.

CHAPTER 2

KEY FEATURES OF THE AMERICAN ECONOMY

The American economy is the largest economy in the world.

The American economy is the world's largest economy by nominal Gross Domestic Product (GDP). The U.S. accounted for 25.4% of the global economy in 2022 in nominal terms. The U.S. dollar is the currency of record most used in international transactions and is the world's reserve currency.[1]

Gross Domestic Product (GDP) of the largest economies

The GDP measures the annual value of all the products and services produced within each country.

By GDP size we have the following selected ranking:

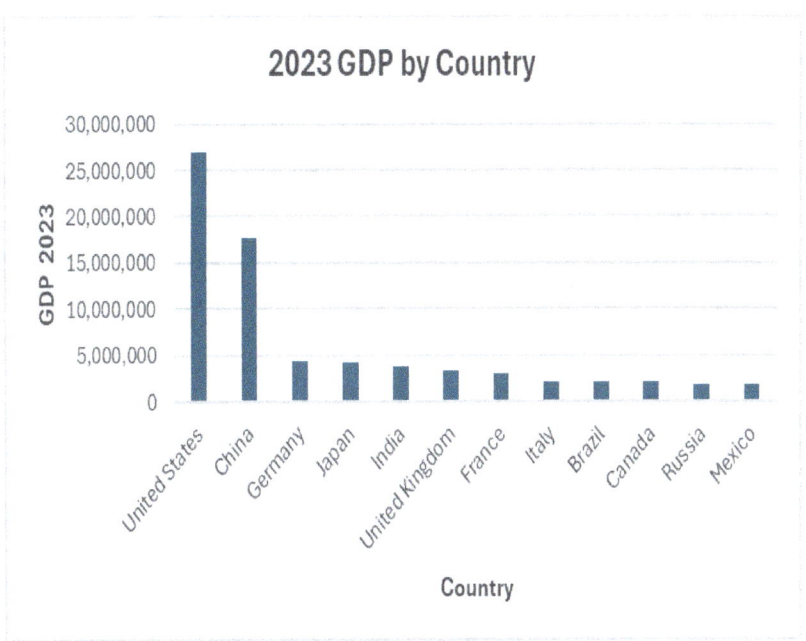

Source: International Monetary Fund

---

[1] "World Economic Outlook Database, April 2022". IMF.org. International Monetary Fund. Retrieved April 20, 2022.
"World Bank Country and Lending Groups". datahelpdesk.worldbank.org. World Bank. Retrieved September 29, 2019.

GDP per capita

To be able to compare countries by GDP, it is usual practice in economics to do so by comparing GDP per capita for each country. This metric is used by economists to gauge the economic prosperity of a country and compare it with others. Essentially, it provides an average value of economic output per person, which can be a useful indicator of a country's standard of living.

GDP per capita is calculated by dividing the nation's GDP by its population. To compare with other nations, the country's gross domestic product (GDP) is measured at purchasing power parity (PPP), which is the value of all final goods and services produced in an economy in a year adjusted for inflation, divided by the average population mid-year.

Under this measurement the US economy is not in first place; nevertheless, Americans have the highest average household and employee income among the Organization for Economic Cooperation and Development (OECD) member states.

Based on this estimate, in 2019, the average GDP per capita (PPP) of all of the countries of the world was $18,381 US Dollars.

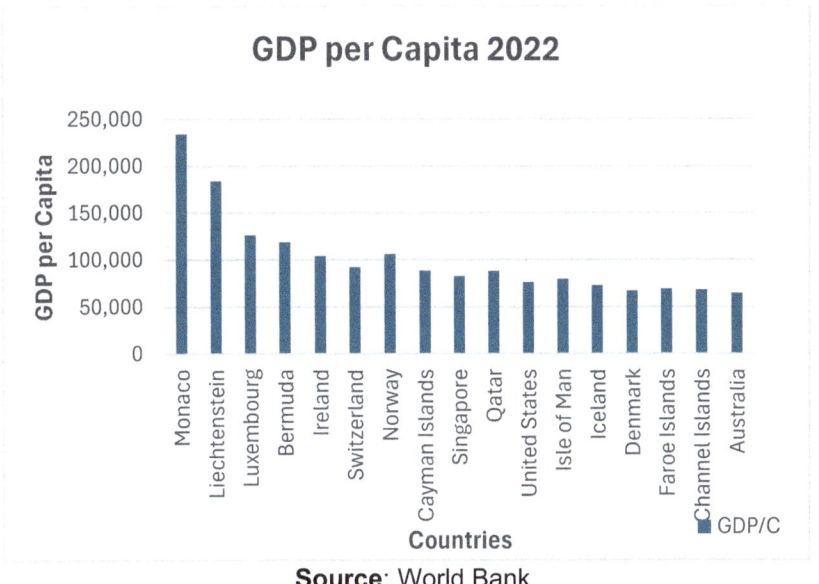

Source: World Bank

In 2023. the per capita estimate for the US was $80,000.

What makes the US economy achieve its size?

The American economy is based on a system of free-enterprise and capitalism.

One of the most important characteristics of capitalism is the existence of private property or property that is owned by individuals or groups. This system emphasizes that individuals are free to own and control the factors of production.

Besides its safe and efficient business environment, in the US there are some of the largest financial institutions and private corporations.

Financial Institutions

The US has the largest stock markets in the world. Of the total world's stock exchanges capitalization in September of

2023, the New York Stock Exchange had a share of 23% and NASDAQ a 20% share.

Four private banks are amongst the 10 largest in the world ranked by capitalization value. Three private insurance companies are also in the top ten largest in the world.

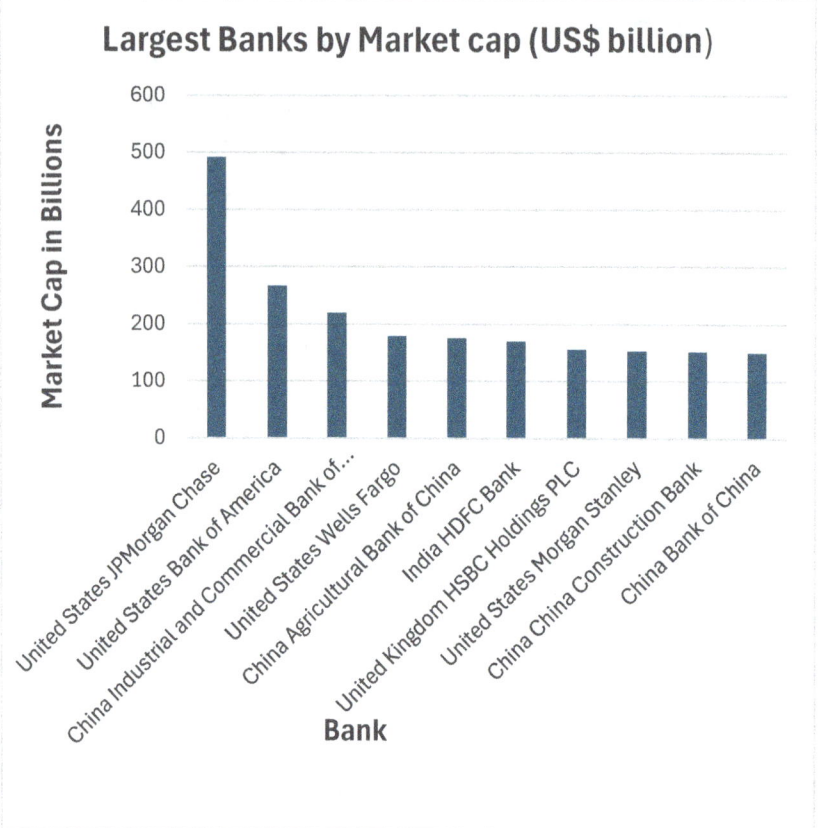

Source: Forbes, https://www.forbesindia.com/article/explainers/the-10-largest-banks-in-the world.

Private Corporations

According to a report from Price Waterhouse Coopers (PwC) of mid-2021, of the top 100 companies in the world, 59 US firms represented 65% of the total world market capitalization value.

More currently (July 2023) the largest Companies by Market Capitalization worth more than a trillion dollars:

Source: https://companiesmarketcap.com/

Note that five of the six largest companies in the world are American (the exception is Saudi Aramco).

By GDP growth from 2000-2020 according to Forbes (08/2021) with data of the Bureau of Economic Analysis (BEA), the top 5 industries in the US were the following:

- Data Processing, Internet publishing and other information services.
- Real Estate
- Insurance Carriers and related activities
- Computer systems design and related services
- Publishing industries, except internet (includes software).

Important world food producer

The US is amongst the four largest food producers in the world (China, India, US & Brazil).[2]

- The US is the largest exporter of Soybeans, with 45% of the market share.
- The US is dominant in the Cotton trade, with 43% of the export market.
- The US is the number one exporter of Corn, with 39% of the export market.
- The US is also the largest exporter of Wheat, with a 15% market share.

Important participant in foreign trade

The U.S. has free trade agreements with several countries, including Canada and Mexico (through the USMCA), Australia, South Korea, Israel, and several others that are in effect or under negotiation.[3]

The United States plays a significant role in global trade. As of 2022, the U.S. ranked as the third-largest global merchandise exporter, contributing 8.1% of the world's total export trade.

In terms of total trade value, the U.S. engages in commerce with more than 200 countries and territories, with exports and imports combined reaching $7.0 trillion[4].

The United States ranks among world-leading nations for exporting refined petroleum oils, petroleum gases and cars. The trade of refined and crude oil in the US is the largest with a market share of 15-18%.

---

[2] FAO Statistical Yearbook 2022 - World Food and Agriculture.
[3] "Report for Selected Countries and Subjects: April 2023". imf.org. International Monetary Fund.
[4] World Bank

US Trade. Imports, Exports and Balance 2023

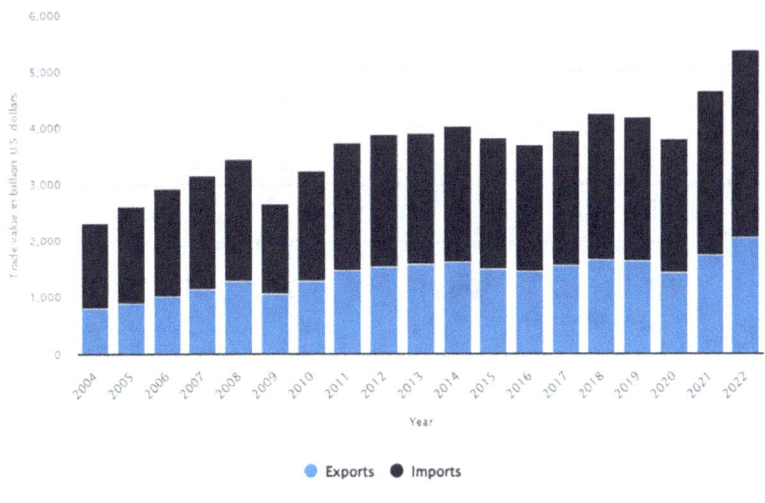

Source: Statista

Significant job creation

One important feature of the American economy is the significant creation of millions of new jobs. **On average (using 2011-2019 period) 2,358,000 new jobs were created every year. That is around 200,000 new jobs on average every month.**

In 2023 according to the U.S. Bureau of Labor Statistics, the ten largest industries by employment in the US were:[5]

1. **Healthcare and Social Assistance**: This sector employs a significant number of people, including doctors, nurses, caregivers, and administrative staff. It plays a crucial role in maintaining public health and well-being.
2. **Professional and Business Services**: From consultants to IT specialists, this sector covers a

---

[5] US Bureau of Labor Statistics, https://www.bls.gov/

broad spectrum. It includes legal services, accounting, management consulting, and more.
3. **Retail Trade**: Retailers, both online and brick-and-mortar, contribute to this sector. Jobs here involve sales, customer service, inventory management, and more.
4. **Manufacturing**: Despite automation, manufacturing still employs a substantial workforce. Jobs range from assembly line workers to engineers.
5. **Leisure and Hospitality**: Think restaurants, hotels, entertainment venues, and tourism. This sector provides jobs in food service, accommodation, and recreation.
6. **Construction**: Construction workers, architects, and engineers contribute to building infrastructure, homes, and commercial spaces.
7. **Financial Activities**: Banking, insurance, real estate, and investment services fall under this category. Jobs include bankers, financial analysts, and real estate agents.
8. **Education Services**: Teachers, professors, and educational administrators work in schools, colleges, and universities.
9. **Transportation and Warehousing**: Truck drivers, logistics experts, and warehouse staff are essential for moving goods across the country.
10. **Other Services**: This catch-all category includes diverse roles like hairdressers, repair technicians, and personal trainers.

The top two employers in the US are:

1. **Walmart**: With a staggering 2.3 million employees, Walmart holds the top spot. Their extensive workforce contributes to their position as a retail giant.

2. **Amazon**: As the second-largest employer, Amazon employs approximately 1.6 million people. Their

online retail, cloud storage, and computing services have made them a global powerhouse.

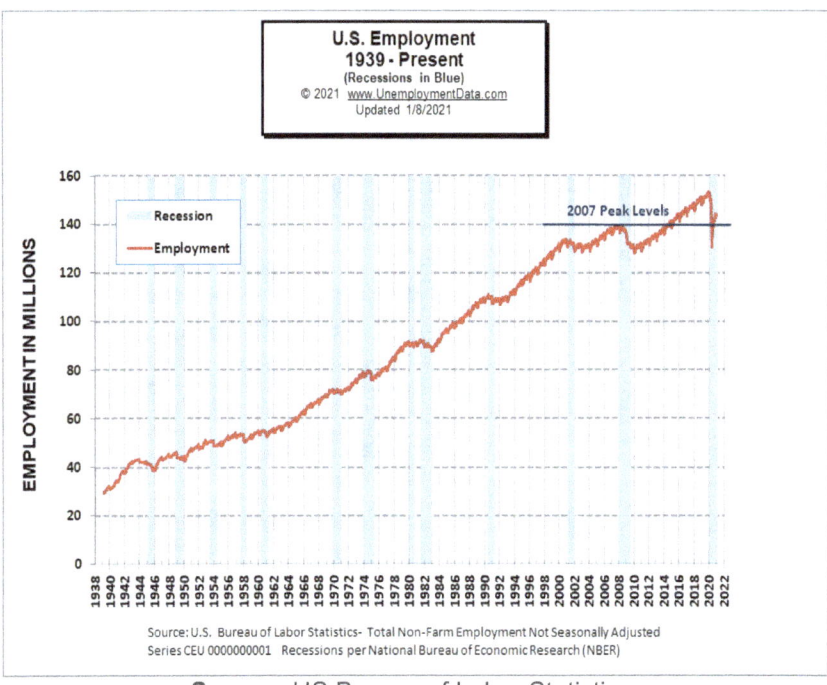

Source: US Bureau of Labor Statistics

Unemployment

Recent average unemployment rate (excluding the Covid pandemic period) has been around 3.9% or less.[6] The unemployment rates for the top 6 largest economies by GDP at the end of 2022 were the following:
Unemployment Rates for the World's Largest Economies
- United States: 3.6%
- China: 4.9%
- Japan: 2.6%
- Germany: 3.0%
- India: 7.3%

---

[6] Bureau of Labor Statistics

- United Kingdom: 3.6%
- France: 7.4%
- Russian Federation: 4.7%

Economic Growth

Since the 1970s the rate of US economic growth has been slowing down (decelerating). The following graph shows the annual rate of real GDP growth for the past 63 years. The red line is the trendline and shows a negative slope (declining) which means that there has been a decline in the annual growth rate and the tendency is negative (continuing to fall).

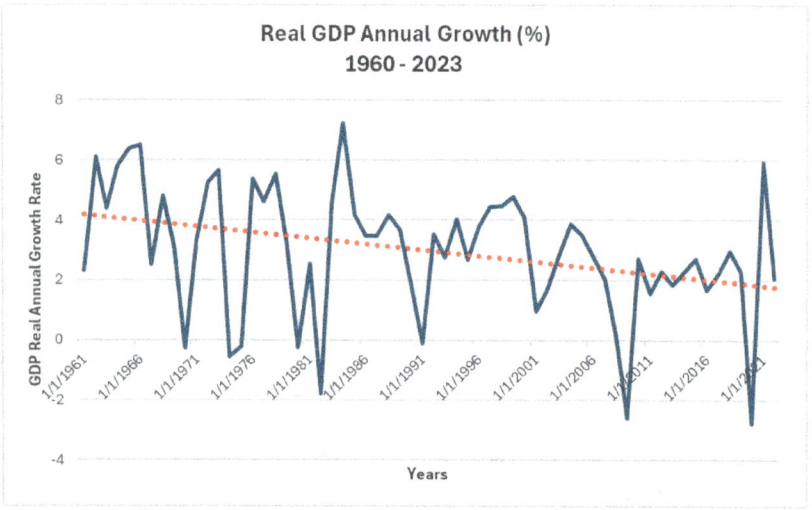

Source: FRED, St Louis Federal Reserve Bank.

The following graph describes the behavior of US real potential GDP annual growth. Potential GDP growth is the Congressional Budget office (CBO's) estimate of the output the economy would produce with a high rate of use of its capital and labor resources. The data is adjusted to remove the effects of inflation. In other words, it shows how much the US economy could grow if all its resources were used without causing inflationary pressures. The graph shows a declining rate of potential growth (red trend line). Both pieces of data, the annual real growth rate, and the potential growth rate, show a declining trend.

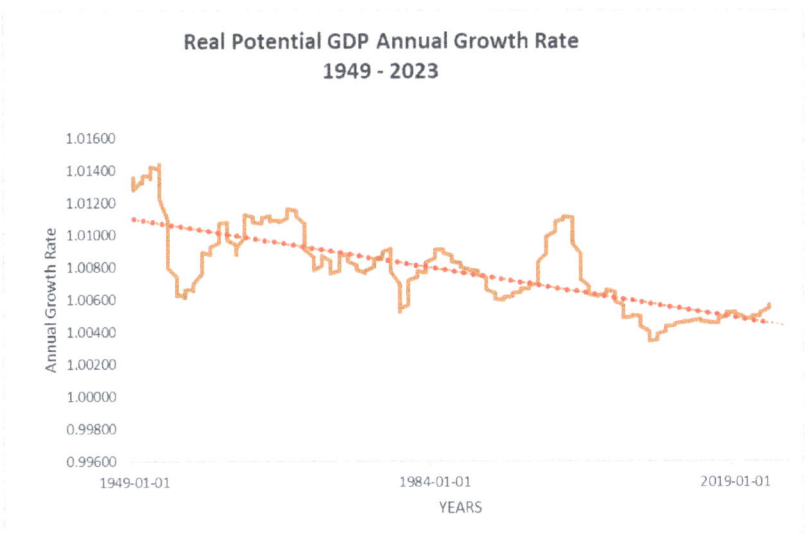

Source: FRED, St Louis Federal Reserve Bank.

In the next 30 years the economy will be facing some strong challenges that can further slow the economy's growth.

CHAPTER 3

US ECONOMIC GROWTH 1970 - 2020

In our book "*Economic Deceleration*", we explained why and how the US economy after having had a history of strong economic growth throughout the 1950-1960s, in the 1970s the average growth trend started slowing down (Decelerating).

In the past 50 years, the US average economic growth rates have been decreasing in the following ways: in the 50's and 60's the average growth rate was above 4 percent; in the 70's and 80's it dropped to around 3 percent. In the last ten years, the average rate has been below 2 percent.

The graph below shows the average GDP growth rate by decade, and a red line indicating the trend.

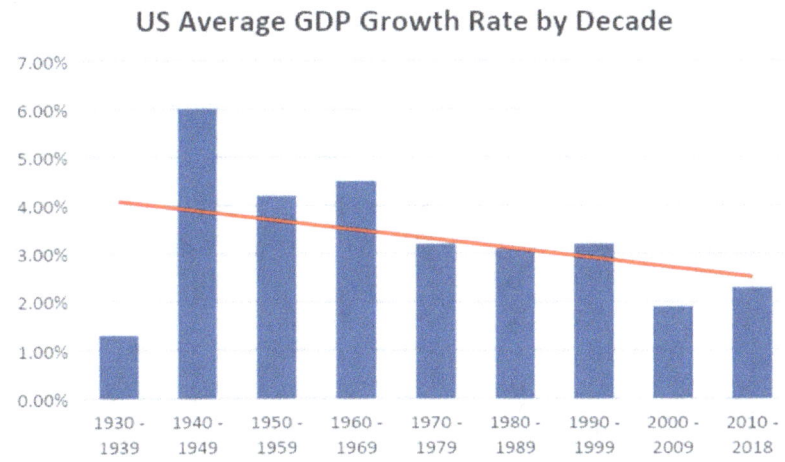

Source: FRED, St Louis Federal Reserve Bank.

<u>The origins of the economic growth deceleration process</u>

The origin of the economic growth deceleration is related to the end of the Bretton Woods International Financial Agreement.[7]

---

[7] The Federal Reserve History, https://www.federalreservehistory.org/

The Bretton Woods agreement was created in a 1944 conference of all the World War II allied nations. It took place in Bretton Woods, New Hampshire.

In this agreement the member countries agreed to keep their currencies fixed to the dollar, and the United States had the responsibility of keeping the dollar price of gold fixed. Since 1958, U.S. dollars were convertible to gold at a fixed exchange rate of $35 an ounce.

In the 1960s, European and Japanese exports became more competitive. The deteriorating U.S. balance of payments, combined with military spending and foreign aid, resulted in a large supply of dollars around the world. Eventually, there were more foreign-held dollars than the United States gold reserves. This made the country vulnerable to a run-on gold.

Many efforts were made to adjust the U.S. balance of payments and to uphold the Bretton Woods system, both domestically and internationally.

International efforts were also made to stem a run-on gold. In this respect, the London Gold Pool was formed on November 1, 1961. The pool consisted of a group of eight central banks. The pool was successful for six years until another gold crisis ensued. The British pound sterling devalued, and another run-on gold occurred, and France withdrew from the pool. The pool collapsed in March 1968.

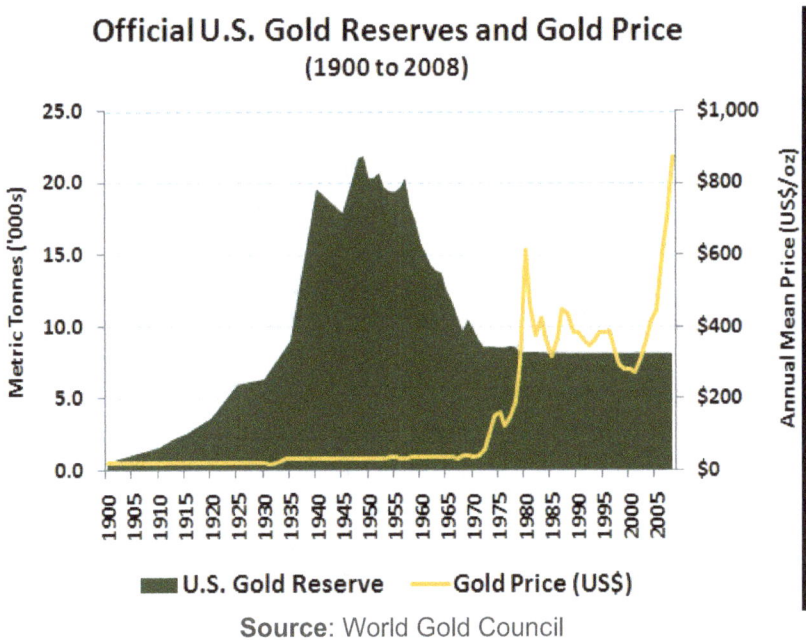

Source: World Gold Council

At that time the seven remaining members of the London Gold Pool agreed to formulate a two-tiered system. The two-tier system was in place until the U.S. gold window closed in 1971.

On the evening of August 15, 1971, President Nixon adopted measures directed to correct economic conditions as well as stopping the loss of gold reserves. As a result of these measures, foreign governments could no longer exchange their dollars for gold.

In 1973, Nixon unhooked the value of the dollar from gold altogether. Without price controls, gold quickly shot up to $120 per ounce on the free market. The Bretton Woods system was over.[8]

---

[8] The price of the dollar went from $35.00 dollars for an ounce of gold at the beginning of 1970, to $455.00 dollars an ounce by 1971

The oil shocks.

During the 1950s and 1960s, industrialized countries were importing increasing amounts of oil to cater to their economies' growing energy requirements. Until this time, the price of the barrel of oil had remained stable for decades.

However, in the early 1970s, the US dollar devaluation negatively affected the oil-exporting countries, because their exports were valued in dollars, and hence the revenue derived from oil exports decreased appreciably[9]. As the oil-exporting countries saw their income reduced, they reacted by updating their prices based on the price of gold[10]. The resulting increase in the price of oil was achieved by reducing the supply of oil through an agreement of the oil exporting countries OPEC (Organization of Petroleum Exporting Countries).

Additionally, in October 1973, a war started between Israel and some Arab countries (the Yom Kippur War), and because the United States supported Israel in this war, the oil-exporting Arab countries (members of OPEC) decided to impose an oil embargo, reducing its total production, and thus quadrupling the price of oil[11].

To make matters worse, a few years later with the start of the Iranian Revolution in 1978, there was a reduction of that country's oil production, further pressuring the oil market and raising prices to unprecedented levels.

---

[9] US Energy Information, Crude Oil Prices, WTI.

[11] Ibid

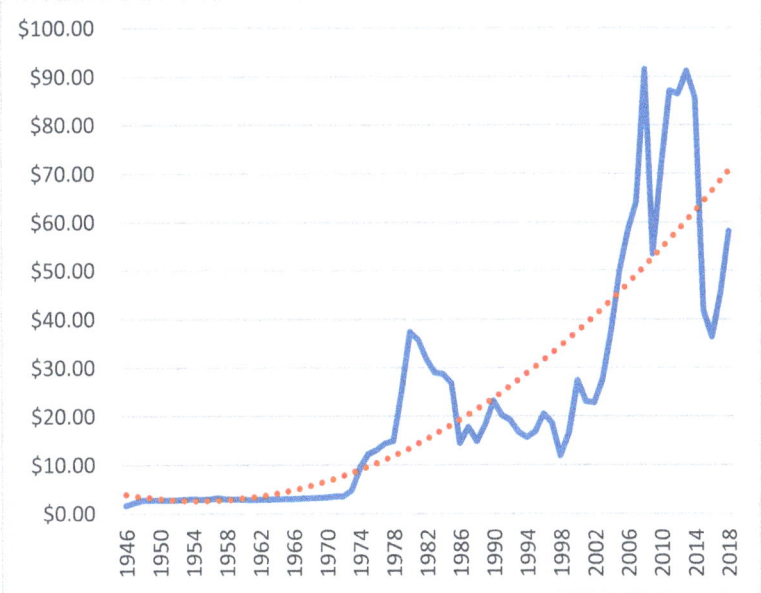

Oil Prices (Dollars per Barrel 1946 to 2018)
(Red Line Indicates the trend line)

Source: FRED, St Louis Federal Reserve Bank, West Texas Intermediate price.

Consequences that affected economic growth

Some of the most powerful consequences resulting from the abandonment of the Bretton Woods Financial System and the oil shock were:

- The American economy entered a process of "Deindustrialization".
- There was a significant loss of wealth, and many developing countries entered a debt crisis during the 1980s.
- It became the beginning of the US balance of trade deficit.

These actions had a major impact on the US and the economies of oil-importing countries. Here we look in more detail at each of the consequences.

Deindustrialization

Deindustrialization is a process of removal or reduction of industrial capacity or activity in a country or region, especially of heavy industry or manufacturing industry. It is the opposite of industrialization.[12]

The process of deindustrialization means loss and/or reduction of the industrial plant (manufacturing sector). In the advanced countries, especially in the United States, the manufacturing plant was reduced as production of manufactured goods was transferred to other countries with cheaper labor costs.

The process of deindustrialization began during the period of high inflation in the United States (1962 to 1978). To maintain its competitiveness, the US shipped many of its manufacturing jobs to countries with abundant labor and low costs (low wages). This process was a general phenomenon followed by other developed countries in different periods and in different degrees.

In a June 1986 publication, Ronald Kutscher and Valerie Personick of the U.S. Bureau of Labor Statistics[13] detailed the manufacturing sectors that lost more production and jobs in the 1970s.

Their research highlighted, among others, the following sectors: textiles, mineral products (iron, steel, copper), tobacco, leather products and rubber, watches, rims, railway equipment, heating equipment, engines, and turbines.

It should be noted that this process of deindustrialization was global and continues to the present day in some

---

[12] IMF, Deindustrialization–Its Causes and Implications, September 1997
[13] Ronald Kutscher and Valerie Personick, *Deindustrialization and the shift to services*. Bureau of Labor Statistics. Monthly Labor Review, June 1986.

manufacturing activities. Consequently, many of the countries that originally benefited from the transfer of these industries are now experiencing the departure of manufacturing plants to other countries with cheaper labor.

One important economic consequence of deindustrialization is the decrease of the economic participation of the manufacturing sector in total GDP. The graph below shows the importance of manufacturing in total production for developed countries over the period of 1960 to 2017. As can be seen, manufacturing participation in GDP decreased from an average of 23% of GDP in 1960 to 9% in 2017.

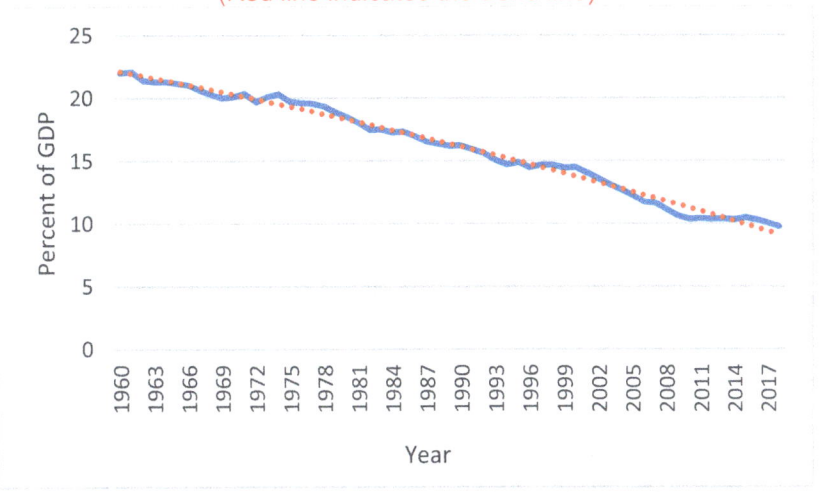

Source: World Bank Data, Manufacturing and GDP

Moving the industrial plant abroad meant many workers were unemployed and caused significant damage to the trade union movement. This influenced wages (promoting wage stagnation).

A result of the decrease in manufacturing activity has been a decrease in employment in the sector. For example, in the US, data from the 1910 Census show that 32 percent of nonfarm jobs were in manufacturing; in 2015, manufacturing accounted for less than 9 percent of total nonfarm employment. The number of people employed in manufacturing was 8 million in 1910, and 12 million in 2015. While employment in manufacturing grew over the past 100 years, employment in other industries grew more[14].

The following graph shows the percentage of the employed labor force working in manufacturing in the US. After WWII, the trend has been towards a decline, with an accelerating rate from the sixties forward.

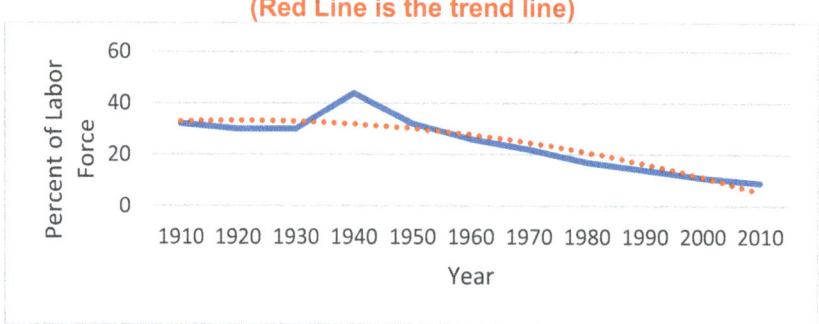

Source: Employment by major industry sector:
U.S. Bureau of Labor Statistics
https://www.bls.gov/emp/.../employment-by-major-industry-sector.htm

Another impact was a massive transfer of wealth from oil importing countries to the OPEC countries and the increased level of international indebtedness of many countries.

Loss of wealth and increased indebtedness

Many Latin American, African and some Asian oil-importing countries, had to borrow large amounts of financial

---

[14] Bureau of Labor Statistics, U.S. Department of Labor, The Economics Daily, Employment by industry, 1910 and 2015 on the Internet at https://www.bls.gov/opub/ted/2016/employment-by-industry-1910-and-2015.htm (visited October 27, 2019).

resources to finance their imports. A large part of the funds used for the loans granted to these countries came from OPEC countries as recycled dollars; as a result, these dollars were called "petrodollars".[15]

The next graph describes the surge of net income that OPEC countries experienced during this time due to the significant increase in the price of oil.

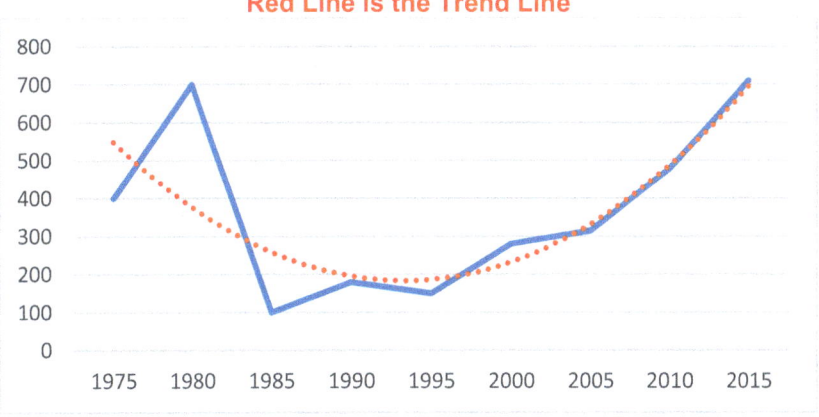

Source: US Energy Information Administration (EIA)

The following graph shows how the debt of oil-importing countries rose as a percentage of their GDP, during the period 1960 to 2010.

Debt service, which is the interest payment on the debt, worsened as interest rates were increased to fight inflation.

---

[15] What is the Petrodollar, Kimberly Amadeo Updated on June 4, 2022, https://www.thebalancemoney.com/what-is-a-petrodollar-3306358

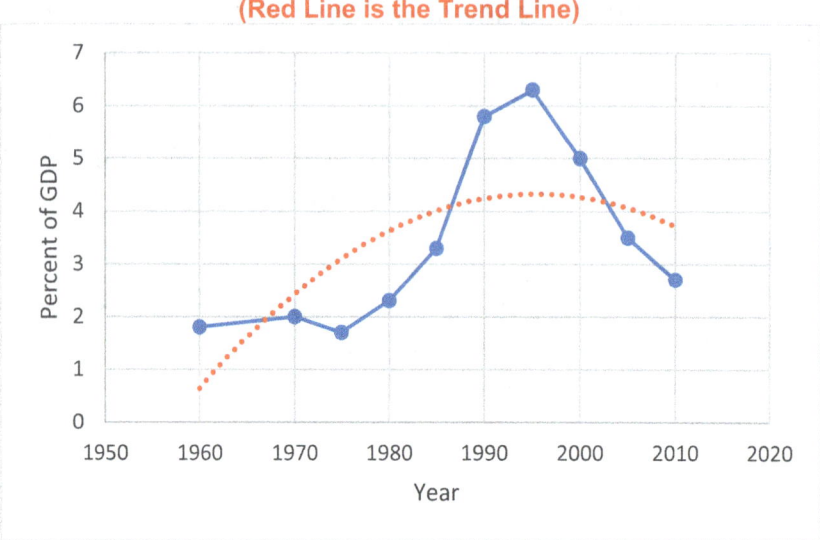

Source: Stephen Kretzmann and Irfan Nooruddin, "An Investigation into the Relationship Between Debt and Oil", Oil Change International.

In the case of Latin American countries, their external debt rose from $12 billion dollars in 1975, to $66 billion dollars in 1982, plus they exhausted additional funding resources[16].

The negative effects were important for all importing countries. For the Latin American economies, the negative impact was so important that the decade of the 1980s was called the ' lost' decade.

It was not until 1989, under the new administration of George H. W. Bush, that the renegotiation of foreign debt of developing countries was facilitated through the so-called "Brady Bonds". This allowed for a global economic recovery during the decade of the 1990s.

---

[16] Joint BIS-IMF-OECD-World Bank statistics on external debt, https://www.bis.org/publ/r_debt.htm

Another impact on the American economy was the surge of its balance of trade deficit.

Balance of trade deficit

Economic growth has been impacted unfavorably by the deficit of the US Balance of Trade (balance of purchases of goods and services from abroad from the sale of US goods and services to foreign countries).

Source: US Census Bureau

For aggregate demand purposes the important concept is net exports, which means the net balance of exports minus imports, also known as the balance of trade.

Since 1971 this deficit has been increasing. Currently, US exports account for about 11% of GDP and Imports around 14.6%. The amount of this deficit (which represents purchases of foreign made goods and services) is subtracted from the aggregate demand.

CHAPTER 4

PRESENT AND FUTURE GROWTH CHALLENGES

To discuss what we see as the future economic growth challenges, we divide this chapter into three subsections, as follows:

- A. Present Growth-Income Challenges.
- B. Future Growth-Demographic Challenges.
- C. Financial Challenges.

A. Present Growth-Income Challenges

Economic growth in the short-term is determined by demand side components that are identified as the Aggregate Demand (levels of Investment, Government Expenses, Net Exports and most importantly by Consumption).

On the consumption part of the demand side of the economy, economic growth is being limited because of the significant income inequality of the working population, where the income of a significant proportion of the population has stagnated in real terms (discounting inflation). As their real income has not grown, they have incurred an increasing level of indebtedness. This has its limits and risks.

Income inequality

In economic terms, income inequality is how income is distributed among individuals, groups, populations, social classes, or countries.

A commonly used measurement is the Gini index, which summarizes the distribution of income into a single number. It ranges from zero, which is a perfectly equal distribution, to one where only one person has 100% of national income. The Gini coefficient applies comparisons across jurisdictions.

- Key global causes for income inequality

Globally there are several factors that have generated greater income inequality, such as the following:

  o Technological innovations

Technological progress can remove numerous jobs by investment in mechanization or increasing the skill criterion for job hiring.

In this respect, educated workers have fared better; the wages received by those who finished their education with a four-year college degree grew from 134% of high school graduates' wages to 168%.

While increasing educational attainment has helped to raise wages for many workers, the majority of Americans have not completed a four-year degree.

  o Trade globalization and decline of labor unions

Many companies have outsourced their high-tech and manufacturing jobs overseas. The United States lost 36% of its factory jobs from 1980 to 2020. These were traditionally higher-paying union jobs. Service jobs have increased, but these are much lower paid.

At the lower pay scales, longer periods of high unemployment have left workers with less leverage when asking for higher pay. More intense competition from foreign firms and a decline in higher-paying manufacturing jobs have also slowed wage growth at the bottom and middle of the wage scale. Falling union membership has weakened the position of working households, as well.

- Government actions

The federal minimum wage provides an important backstop to declining wages, but policymakers have failed to maintain its real (inflation-adjusted) value over time.

- Workers' compensation

Inequality has grown as incomes have risen dramatically at the top of the scale, while rising only modestly or even stagnating in the middle and bottom scales.

Among the reasons for this is the way workers get compensated. The workers (labor) at the bottom of the pay scale earn hourly wages that get adjusted mainly by minimum salary and/or inflation adjustments.

In the middle scale the employees earn salaries that not only increase annually for inflation, but that might also include annual pay grade improvements.

The top executives and specialists earn higher incomes as their payments are determined by what they do, with some bonuses included.

- <u>Income inequality in the US</u>

The U.S. Census Bureau measures income inequality using household income. One common way of measuring income inequality is to rank all households by income, from lowest to highest, and then to divide all households into five groups with equal numbers of people, known as **quintiles**. This calculation allows for measuring the distribution of income among the five groups compared to the total.

The first quintile is the lowest fifth or 20%, the second quintile is the next lowest, and so on. Income inequality can be measured by comparing what share of the total income is earned by each quintile.

Income Distribution Range in the US in 2022

Quintile	Income Range
Lowest quintile	0 - 28,000
Second quintile	28,001 - 56,000
Middle quintile	56,001 - 93,000
Fourth quintile	93,001 - 154,000
Highest quintile	154,001 +

Source: Statista, https://www.statista.com/statistics/203183/percentage-distribution-of-household-income-in-the-us/

Sluggish and uneven wage growth has been cited as a key factor behind widening income inequality in the United States.

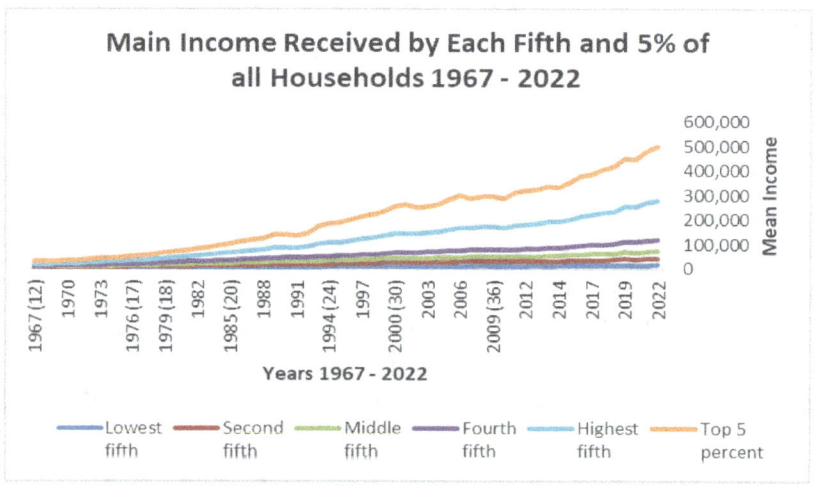

Source: US Census Bureau, Historical Income Tables.

Income inequality continues to worsen in the US

In 2020 the Census Bureau reported that income inequality in the United States had reached its highest level in 50 years, the U.S. Gini index, was 0.489.

Household Income Distribution by Percentiles 1967 – 2022

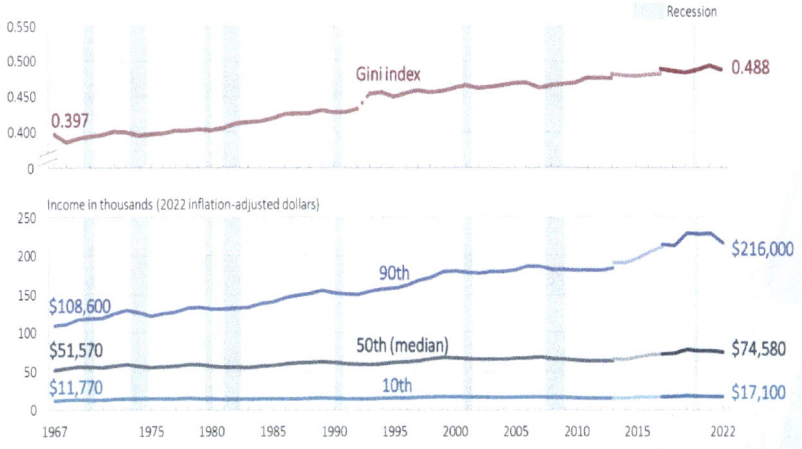

Source: U.S. Census Bureau, Current Population Survey, 1968 to 2022

The earnings of the top 0.1% surged from $648,725 in 1979 to nearly $2.9 million in 2019, an increase of 345%.

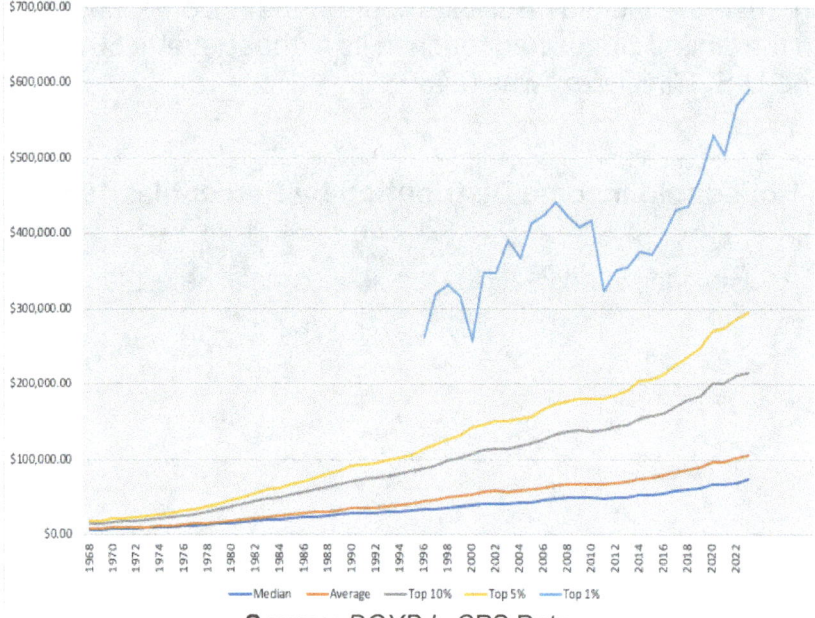

Source: *DQYDJ* , CPS Data

Over time, from the late 1960s to the early 1980s, the top fifth of the income distribution typically received between about 43% to 44% of all income. Since then, the share of income that the top fifth received began to rise. One important reason is the growth of investment income.[17]

- Greater impact of investment income

Income from investments, such as capital gains, dividends, interest, and rent, goes primarily to high-income households, so the growth in investment income as a share of overall income has widened the gap between the wealthy and everyone else.

---

[17] Pew Research Center February 7, 2020, 6 Facts About Economic Inequality in The U.S.

Between 2000 and 2021, asset price inflation created about $160 trillion in "paper wealth". Valuations of assets like equity and real estate grew faster than real economic output. In aggregate, the global balance sheet grew 1.3 times faster than GDP. It quadrupled to reach $1.6 quintillion in assets, consisting of $610 trillion in real assets, $520 trillion in financial assets outside the financial sector, and $500 trillion within the financial sector.[18]

Another reason is the increasing cost of benefits.

- Increasing cost of benefits

Cash money isn't the only way workers are compensated, of course health insurance, retirement account contributions, tuition reimbursement, transit subsidies, and other benefits all can be part of the package. But wages and salaries are the biggest (about 70%, according to the Bureau of Labor Statistics) and most visible component of employee compensation.

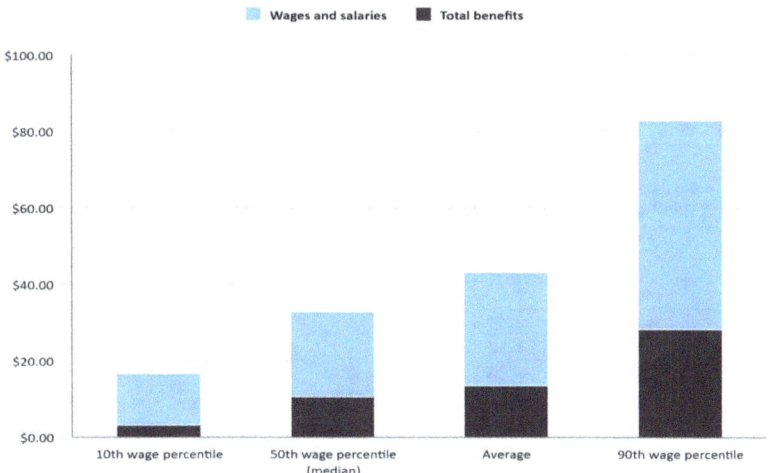

Wages and Total Benefits by Wage Percentile 2023

Source: Bureau of Labor Statistics, Employer Costs for Employee Compensation

---

[18] Mc Kinsey & Co.

One theory is that rising benefit costs – particularly employer-provided health insurance – may be constraining employers' ability or willingness to raise cash wages. According to the Bureau of Labor Statistics generated compensation cost indices, total benefit costs for all civilian workers have risen an inflation-adjusted 22.5% since 2001 (when the data series began), versus 5.3% for wage and salary costs.

- How does income inequality affect the economy?

Wage inequality reduces economic growth by shifting resources toward wealthy savers rather than lower- and middle-class spenders. Since the wealthy tend to save nearly 50% of their marginal income while the remainder of the population saves roughly 10%, it is estimated that this would reduce annual consumption (the largest component of GDP) by as much as 5%.

Also, the increasing cost of benefits, like health insurance, requires increasing amounts of disposable income for the same benefits, therefore further reducing the households' purchasing power.

Median US Household Income vs Purchasing Power in 2010 Dollars

Year	Median U.S. Household Income1	Annual average index value, CPI-U U.S. city average all items index	Ratio of base index value to yearly index value	Ratio equals	Median U.S. Household Income, constant 2010 dollars
2010	$49,276.00	218.06	218.06 / 218.06 =	1	$49,276.00
2011	$50,054.00	224.94	218.06 / 224.94 =	0.97	$48,552.38
2012	$51,017.00	229.59	218.06 / 229.59 =	0.95	$48,466.15
2013	$53,585.00	232.96	218.06 / 232.96 =	0.94	$50,369.90
2014	$53,657.00	236.74	218.06 / 236.74 =	0.92	$49,364.44
2015	$56,516.00	237.02	218.06 / 237.02 =	0.92	$51,994.72
2016	$59,039.00	240.01	218.06 / 240.01 =	0.91	$53,725.49
2017	$61,136.00	245.12	218.06 / 245.12 =	0.89	$54,411.04
2018	$63,179.00	251.11	218.06 / 251.11 =	0.87	$54,965.73
2019	$68,703.00	255.66	218.06 / 255.66 =	0.85	$58,397.55
2020	$68,010.00	258.81	218.06 / 258.81 =	0.84	$57,128.40
2021	$70,784.00	270.97	218.06 / 270.97 =	0.8	$56,627.20

Source: St. Louis FED, FRED database, MEHOINUSA672N

The current real average wage (that is, the average hourly wage after accounting for inflation) for non-management private-sector workers has about the same purchasing power it did 40 years ago. And what wage gains there have been have mostly flowed to the highest-paid tier of workers[19].

As many workers have an income that doesn't grow, access to credit may be the driving factor in growing household debt. The credit limits are determined by the consumer's income level, hence affecting the lower pay scale workers more.

- o What other way does current income inequality affect the future?

In 1931, historian James Truslow Adams wrote in his book *The Epic of America* that the American dream is "of a land in which life should be better and richer and fuller for everyone, with opportunity for each according to ability or achievement," and "regardless of the fortuitous circumstances of birth or position."

His American dream became reality after World War II as America's middle class grew, almost everyone's income rose, and their children did even better than they did. Americans born in the early 1940s had a 92% chance of obtaining a higher household income than their parents, once they became adults. They would live out the American dream.

But Americans born in the 1980s have only a 50-50 probability at doing better than their parents.

A Wall Street Journal/NORC poll found that only 36% of voters said the American dream still holds true. This was down from 53% and 48% in similar polls in 2012 and 2016,

---

[19] Understanding America's Income Inequality and Its Causes Fuente-PEW RESEARCH CENTER-AUGUST 7, 2018- BY DREW DESILVER

respectively. A typical U.S. family had a slightly lower net worth in 2019 than a typical family in 2001[20].

David Leonhardt wrote in his new book about the fading of the American dream, "Ours was the shining future." "There has not been such a long period of wealth stagnation since the Great Depression," he wrote.[21]

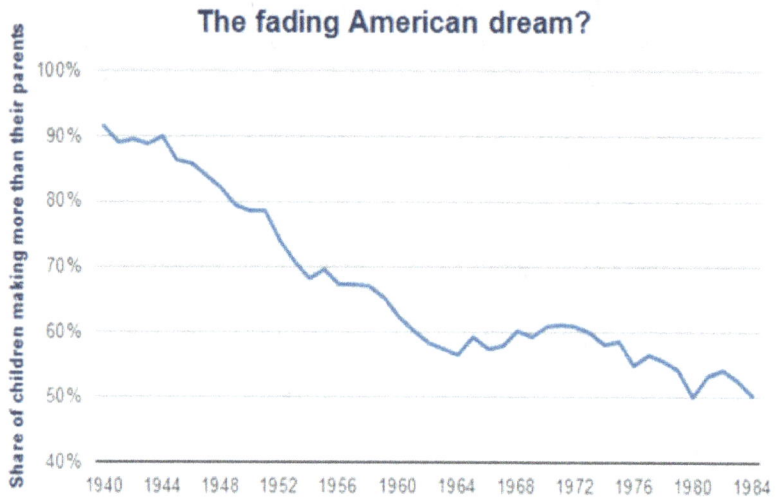

Source: David Leonhardt, The Fading American Dream, Trends in Absolute Income

B. Future Growth-Demographic Challenges

The long-term components that determine economic growth are determined by the supply side components:
- Accumulation of capital stock
- Increases in labor inputs, such as workers or hours worked.

20

https://s.wsj.net/public/resources/documents/WSJ_NORC_Partial_Oct_2023.pdf

[21] David Leonhardt, Ours Was the Shining Future: The Story of the American Dream, Random House (October 24, 2023)

- Level of Productivity - In economics, productivity measures output per unit of input, such as labor, capital, or any other resource.

Future growth projections

We estimate that during the end of the 2020s and early 2030s, economic growth will be favorably impacted by the investments derived from the Chips Act and the Infrastructure Act. This should allow for an average additional growth increase of 1%.

Nevertheless, for the longer term, current projections from the Congressional Budget Office (CBO) and of the Federal Reserve Bank (FED) expect for the next decades the economic growth rate to continue slowing down to an average of 1-1.5%.

Growth of Real Potential GDP and its Components

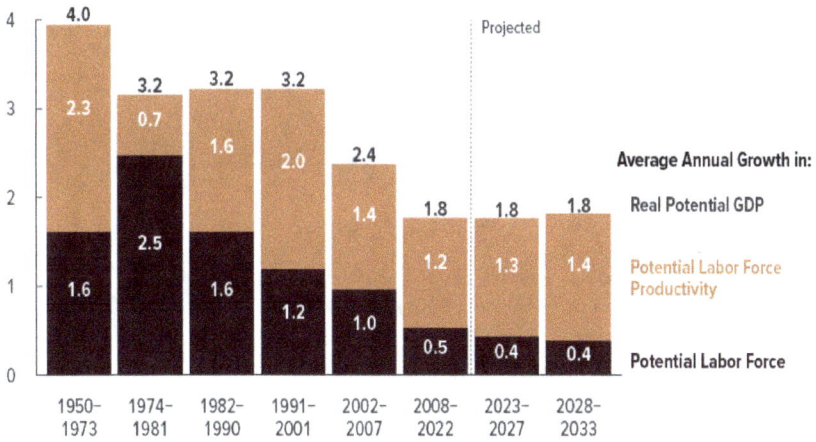

Source: FED – CBO Projections

The economy's potential output is projected to grow much more slowly, on average, over the 2028–2033 period than it did in the second half of the 20th century, mainly because of an ongoing, long-term slowdown in the growth of the labor force as well as slower growth of productivity.

These projections are based among other factors on the expectations for the long-term components that determine economic growth. Let us look at each component and evaluate their outlook.

- Capital accumulation outlook.

This factor is measured by increases in Net Investment as a share of Gross Domestic Product (GDP). The ratio is important because it tells us the amount of new investment available to increase the economy's productive capacity.

This coefficient has declined from 1947 to 2018 from almost 12% to a range of 2-3%.

- What caused this decline?
    - Globalization and deindustrialization were the causes of an important amount of investment migrating to other countries.
    - New technologies are less capital intensive, but their rate of depreciation has been accelerating.
    - A high level of debt and higher interest rates have increased debt service and reduced capital investment.
    - Other explanations include the use of a significant amount of investable funds on stock repurchases and/or Mergers and Acquisitions.

- Industry concentration

Recent studies show that in the US industries are becoming more concentrated and the result of this phenomenon is creating quasi-monopoly profits for concentrated industries and reducing consumer welfare. More than 75% of US industries have experienced an increase in concentration levels over the last two decades[22]. Firms in industries with the largest increases in product market concentration have enjoyed higher profit margins, positive abnormal stock returns, and more profitable Mergers and Acquisitions (M&A) deals, suggesting that market power is becoming an important source of value. Lax enforcement of antitrust regulations and increasing technological barriers to entry appear to be important factors behind this trend. These findings are robust to the inclusion of private firms and factors that account for foreign competition, as well as the use of alternative measures of concentration. Overall, the findings suggest that the nature of US product markets has undergone a structural shift that has weakened competition. A recent study published by University of Chicago Booth School of Business[23], concludes that the data reveals a persistent rise in the dominance of the top 1 percent and top 0.1 percent of businesses in the US. From 1918 to 1975, the Statistics of Income (SOI) produced by the Internal Revenue Service (IRS) provided size groups sorted by net income (green line with circles). Starting in 1959, the Statistics of Income (SOI) also provided size groups sorted by sales (red line with diamonds). The longest and most comprehensive size groups are sorted by assets, available since 1931 (blue line with triangles). No matter the measure you choose, the long-run increase in corporate concentration is clear.

---

[22] Gustavo Grullon, Yelena Larkin and Roni Michaely, Are US Industries Becoming More Concentrated?, April 2020.
[23] Yueran Ma, ProMarket, The publication of the Stigler Center at The University of Chicago Booth School of Business, April 21, 2022.

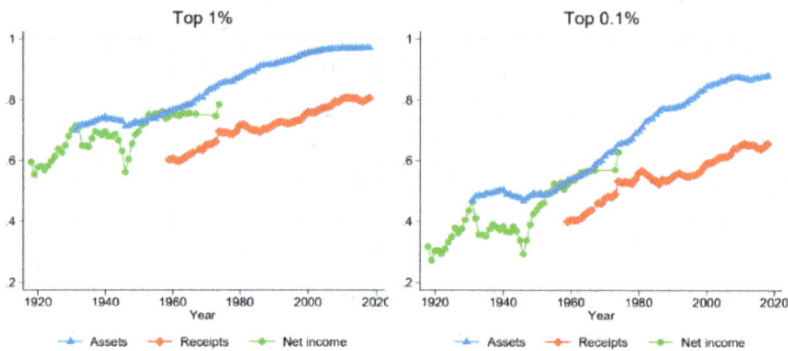

The possibility of a significant growth of net investment will be determined among others, by the future domestic industrial policies; by important growth of US exports (more goods sold to foreign markets); and, most probable, by the capital intensity of the future new technologies.

Technological improvements - Productivity outlook

In the past four decades, the most significant component affecting economic growth has been the drop of productivity.

- What is productivity?

In economics, productivity is a measure of economic performance that compares how much output can be produced with a given set of inputs. Productivity increases when more output is produced with the same number of inputs or when the same amount of output is produced with less inputs.

This component is key to future growth, so understanding why it has been decreasing is fundamental to evaluate its prospects.

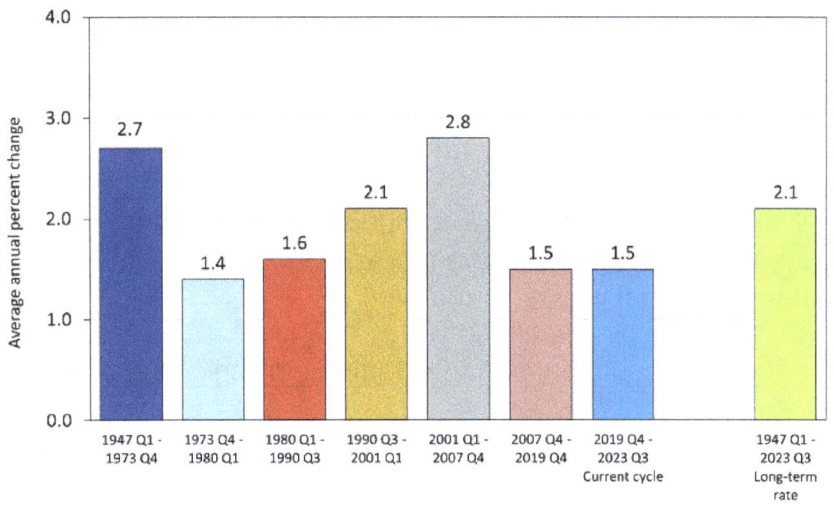

Productivity began falling in the 1970s but has shown a greater fall, particularly since 2004.

- What caused this decline?

Several variables explain the fall in productivity, among them:

➢ One reason is that we are not measuring productivity correctly. While measuring the output of physical goods is more straightforward, the measuring of the output of services is more complicated.

➢ Another reason has to do with low investment due to limits on consumption due to the unequal distribution of income, because an increasing share of income goes to high income households that save most of it and invest it in financial assets.

> With respect to human capital, the average education level in the US has slowed down. Slower growth in prime age labor force tends to coincide with slower growth in productivity. The aging workforce can also slow productivity by making it more difficult to adopt new innovations and processes.[24]

While in recent decades productivity has been the most impactful on growth, in the future demographic changes will have the most impact on growth.

Labor force outlook - **worldwide demographic changes**

Since the last century the world has been going through a profound demographic transformation: the changes include a drop of the fertility rate, that is, the average number of births per woman is dropping across much of the world, as well as the increasing longevity of the population, which means that an increasing share of the population is aging.[25]

- Falling fertility rate

The replacement rate for the population to maintain its size, is at 2.1 children per woman. In 2000 the world's fertility rate was 2.7 births per woman. Currently it's 2.3 births and falling.

Americans now have fewer children than past generations did. And depending on the levels of immigration, the country's population may plateau in the coming decades.

Take a look at this chart, based on census data collected by the demographer William Frey[26]. It shows what would happen to the U.S. population in four different scenarios. In each one, the population eventually peaks. But how soon it

---

[24] The economist 06/03/2023
[25] WAPO 02/23/2023-Min Joo Kim.
[26] Paul Krugman, The New York Times, 03/20/24, "Are Immigrants the Secret to America's Economic Success?"

happens depends on how much immigration the country has:

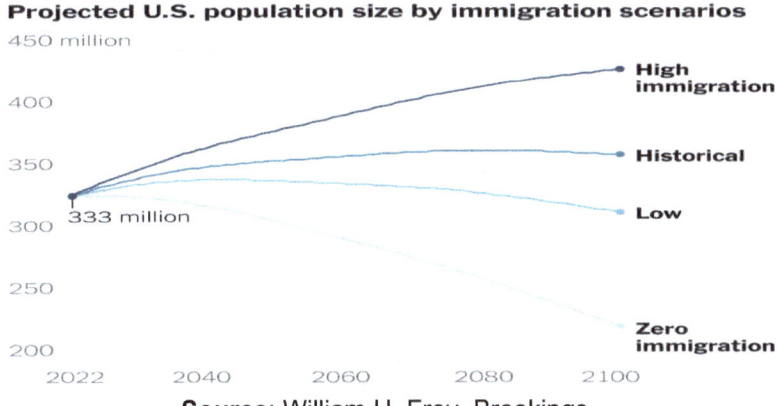

Source: William H. Frey, Brookings.

Although the aggregate Total Fertility Rate (TFR) for some countries remains high, such as, more than 4.5 children per woman in Africa and the Near East, in other nations like China, Italy, Japan France Russia, South Korea, and Thailand, among others, fertility rates are presently below replacement level.[27]

In 2010, 98 countries and territories recorded fertility rates below 2.1. By 2021 the number had grown to 124. By 2030 it can reach 136.

Dramatic examples of this trend are South Korea whose fertility rate fell to 0.78 in 2022. That marks the seventh year of decline. Japan has a rate of 1.3 and the US under 1.7.[28]

In 2020 and 2021, Russia's population declined as deaths exceeded births by 1.7 million. South Korea's population of 52 million recorded in 2022 more deaths (373,000) than

---

[27] Ibid
[28] The economist 06/03/2023-The old & the zestless.

births (249,000). An example of the impact of these trends is the closing of public schools in Korea.[29]

Although Africa in general has the highest fertility rates in the world, these rates are falling more quickly than expected.[30]

Some countries have tried to persuade people to have more children. Those attempts, in Hungary, Sweden, Singapore and elsewhere, have generally failed. They appear to get people to have children earlier, but not to have more kids.

Demographers expect the world's population to peak in the coming decades — likely around 10 billion in the 2080s, according to experts at the United Nations (U.N.).[31]
The other demographic trend is greater longevity.

- <u>Population aging</u>

Globally people are living longer. The United Nations (UN) has projected that the global life expectancy increased from 47 years in 1950, to more than age 65 by 2010 and it expects to reach age 75 by 2050. The reason we are living longer has to do with the development of vaccines and advances in medicine.

It is projected globally that the number of elderlies will increase from 6.9% of the world's population in 2000, to 19.3% by 2050. For the developed regions, persons aged 60 and over will represent one third of the population, while in developing nations they will represent one fifth.

According to PEW Research Center, individuals 65 and older will increase from 531 million in 2010, to 1.5 billion in 2050.

---

[29] The economist 03/11/2023
[30] The economist 04/08/2023-Africa's slowing baby boom
[31] World Population Prospects 2022

Presently, in Japan almost a third of the population is over 65, while in the US its around 17%.

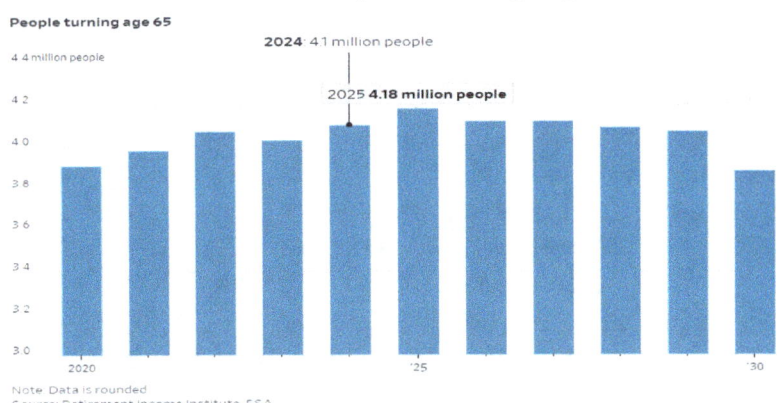

Source: US Census Bureau

- General implications of the aging population

There are several implications: increased dependency, greater need for pensions and health care.

- Increased dependency ratio

Countries with large elderly populations depend on smaller pools of workers to fund with their tax payments the higher health costs, pension benefits and other publicly funded programs.

This results from the fact that in many nations, the population in working ages of 15-64 is decreasing. For example, in China currently every year there are about 32 million fewer people of working age (15-64), while in the US it is 1.4 million.[32] Also, retirement of an increasing share of the labor force means there are fewer people working.

---

[32] https://worldpopulationreview.com/country-rankings/age-dependency-ratio-by-country.

- **Increasing need for pensions and health care**

The need for these benefits is growing further because of the population's increasing longevity. According to the OECD study the effective labor market retirement age for men in the US is 64.9 and for women 64.7. Men are expected to spend 18.6 years in retirement, while women will be 21.3 years[33].

This means that in the following years there will be a greater need for Social Security pension benefits and health care programs (Medicare, Medicaid, and for the Childrens Health Insurance Program as well as outlays for health insurance subsidies under the Affordable Care Act) which have a major impact on the Federal Budget.

According to the Congressional Budget Office (CBO) projections, spending on Social Security will increase as a percentage of GDP over the next three decades. The number of Social Security beneficiaries will increase from 66 million (one fifth of the population) in 2022, to 77 million in 2032 and then to 97 million by 2052 (over one quarter of the projected population).[34]

Total outlays increase from 23.7 percent of GDP in 2023 to 29.0 percent in 2053 in CBO's projections. Rising interest costs and growth in spending on the major health care programs, particularly Medicare, and on Social Security are significant drivers of that increase.

---

[33] OECD (n.d.), "Ageing and Employment Policies", Working Better with Age reports on Denmark, France, Japan, Korea, Netherlands, Norway, Poland, Switzerland, and the United States, https://doi.org/10.1787/19901011.

[34] CBO, Analysis of CBO's June 2023 Long-Term Budget Outlook, JUN 28, 2023.

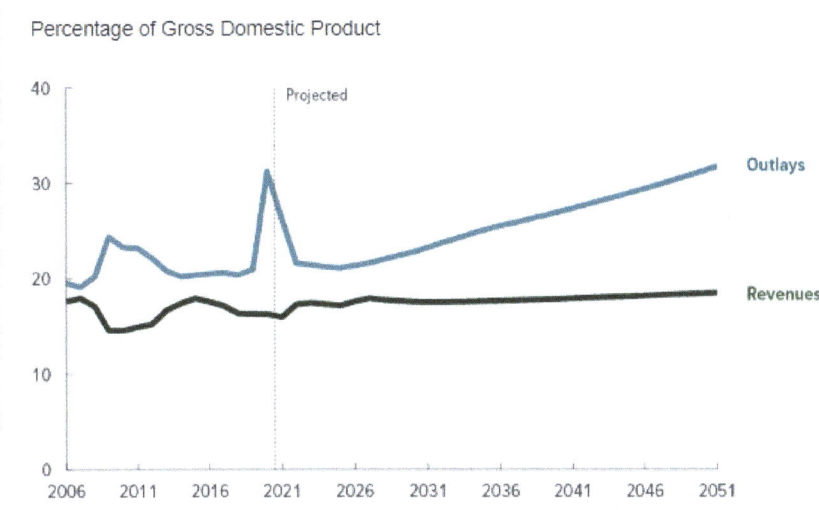

Source: Congressional Budget Office Projections.

In CBO's projections, rising spending on Social Security and Medicare boosts mandatory outlays, but total discretionary spending falls in relation to GDP. As the cost of financing the nation's debt grows, outlays for net interest increase substantially.

- <u>The economic impact of these demographic trends</u>

Economic growth will slow down due to the following:

> ➢ The labor force will grow at a slower rate, while more workers will retire due to aging. This trend will affect the creation of fewer new jobs and therefore potentially fewer additional goods and services will be produced.

> ➢ The growing needs of the ageing population will require a greater number of financial resources allocated to them.

> A greater percentage of the population will be retired and have less discretionary income to spend as they will be dependent on Social Security and/or pensions.

The Federal Reserve (FED) projected that the US potential GDP growth rate will drop from 3% to 2%, due to the aging of population.

Conclusions:

With respect to the most probable outlook of net private investment as a percentage of GDP, we don't expect changes to that ratio due to the continued economic slowdown; to the higher depreciation of new investments; and due to less capital-intensive investments.

With respect to the potential of reversing the fall in productivity, it is possible but not certain, as it depends on the impact of future technological change. So far, we have seen the development of technology for the service sector and the difficulty in measuring its productivity impact. Since productivity changes might continue to be related to the digital revolution, adoption by an aging labor force will be slower.

According to CBO's projections, the US total population will increase from 342 million in 2024, to 383 million people by 2054. The age 65 or older population will outpace the growth of younger age groups.

With respect to the growth of the US population, currently it is mainly (70%) due to net immigration. By 2040 net immigration will account for all (100%) of the population growth.

Since immigration has its limits and technological improvements are unpredictable, future economic growth will be mostly impacted by the shrinking growth of the labor force, as the population will continue to age, and an increasing proportion of the labor force will be retiring.

- Beyond 2050

Nations have started to experience shrinking populations. Examples are Japan and Italy. Presently, millions of "ghost homes" sit empty in rural Japan. Small towns in Japan are on the verge of collapse as their population ages and young people move to cities. Many homes have been left empty after the owners died or people simply moved away.

Before the end of this century the number of people on the planet could shrink. The root cause is a slump in births. As the old die and are not replaced, populations are likely to shrink. Outside of Africa the world's population is forecast to peak in the 2050's and then begin to decrease. But even in Africa the fertility rate is falling fast.

C. FINANCIAL CHALLENGES

Globally there is an increase in indebtedness. The level of debt is increasing in every country and in every sector.

This situation can limit the availability of financial resources for investments in productive activities. Most worrisome is that significant amounts of resources are being loaned for risky financial operations which increases the economy's financial fragility.

Three main types of debt contribute to the challenge: public debt, corporate debt and finally, household debt.

Growing global government debt

Global Public Debt has been increasing in most economies even before 2008, and it worsened even further as the Great Recession caused a drop in tax revenues and a rise in social-welfare payments. From 2008 to mid-2017, global government debt more than doubled, reaching $60 trillion.[35]

China alone accounts for more than one-third of global debt growth since the crisis. Its total debt has increased by more than five times over the past decade to reach $29.6 trillion by mid-2017. Its debt has gone from 145 percent of GDP in 2007, to 256 percent in 2017.

Among Organization for Economic Cooperation and Development countries, government debt now exceeds annual GDP in Japan, Greece, Italy, Portugal, Belgium, France, Spain, and the United Kingdom.

Public debt across all emerging economies is more modest, at 46 percent of GDP on average compared with 105 percent in advanced economies.[36]

Top 10 Countries with the Highest Debt-to-GDP Ratios (%)

Country	Debt to GDP Ratio (%)
Japan	264%
Venezuela	241%
Sudan	186%
Greece	173%
Singapore	168%
Eritrea	164%
Lebanon	151%
Italy	142%
United States	129%
Cape Verde	127%

Source: IMF World Economic Outlook Database, December 2022

---

[35] National post-06/01/2021
[36] Susan Lund, Asheet Mehta, James Manyika, and Diana Goldshtein), August 29, 2018 | Executive Briefing

Increasing corporate debt

Corporate debt as a share of GDP has been steadily increasing. **Global nonfinancial corporate debt, including bonds and loans, more than** doubled over the past decade to hit $86.1 trillion in mid-2022.

In a departure from the past, two-thirds of the growth in corporate debt has come from developing countries. This poses a potential risk, particularly when that debt is in foreign currencies.

China has been the biggest driver of this growth. From 2007 to 2017, Chinese companies added $15 trillion in debt. China now has one of the highest corporate-debt ratios in the world.

The amount of U.S. corporate debt set to mature through 2025 and rated by S&P Global Ratings has climbed to $5.418 trillion following a record $1.1 trillion in bond issuance in the first half of 2020, the rating agency said. It is important to note that in the US corporate lending from banks has been nearly flat since the crisis, while corporate bond issuance has soared. Nonbank lenders, including private-equity funds and hedge funds (known as Shadow Banks) have also become major sources of credit as banks have repaired their balance sheets.[37]

US household debt

US households amassed roughly $16.9 trillion in household debt nationwide by the fourth quarter of 2022. According to

---

[37] https://www.spglobal.com/marketintelligence/en/news-insights/latest-news-headlines/us-corporate-debt-maturing-through-2025-swells-to-5-4-trillion-8211-s-p-59876333#:~:text=The%20amount%20of%20U.S.%20corporate%20debt%20set%20to,first%20half%20of%202020%2C%20the%20rating%20agency%20said.

population figures from the Census Bureau, this is equivalent to around $128,824 per household, on average.[38]

Total household debt increased by approximately $1.1 trillion, or roughly 6.7% since the beginning of 2022.

According to the Federal Reserve Bank of New York, household debt reached an unprecedented high at the beginning of 2023. However, after adjusting for inflation, it is still below the peak of $17.4 trillion in Q4 of 2008, just before the Great Recession.

Over 70% of current debt comes from mortgage debt, which has historically accounted for most of the household debt.

For various reasons, home ownership rate has dropped from its 2007 high of 68 percent to 64 percent in 2018—and while mortgage debt has remained relatively flat, student debt and auto loans went up sharply.

Student loan debt has also been increasing quicker than different types of debt over the past two decades. This debt was relatively small compared to other debt types in 2003 but has since grown significantly and is now the second-largest component of household debt. In the United States, 40 percent of adults surveyed by the Federal Reserve System said they would struggle to cover an unexpected expense of $400. One-quarter of nonretired adults have no pension or retirement savings.

Outstanding student loans now top $1.6 trillion, exceeding credit-card debt—and unlike nearly all other forms of debt, they cannot be discharged in bankruptcy. Auto loans (including subprime auto loans) have also grown rapidly in the United States. [39]

---

[38] What is the state of household debt in the US? (usafacts.org)
[39] https://www.forbes.com/advisor/student-loans/average-student-loan-debt-

Another area of concern is the level of health care debt.

- Health care debt

A Kaiser Family Foundation (KFF) analysis of the 2020 Survey of Income and Program Participation (SIPP) found that one in ten adults in the U.S. have significant medical debt ("significant" is defined as medical debt of over $250) and that U.S. adults owe at least $195 billion in medical debt. Also, a KFF Health Care Debt Survey found that 41% of adults currently have some debt caused by medical or dental bills.[40]

For individuals, these rising – and sometimes unexpected – health care costs can often lead to debt. The problem in quantifying health care debt is that individuals often use other forms of borrowing or debt, such as payment plans, credit cards, bank loans, and borrowing from family and friends to pay their medical and dental bills. These forms of debt are sometimes not included in estimates of medical debt from other surveys and administrative data.

Adults with health care debt report making several sacrifices and enduring substantial financial consequences. Most report cutting back on household spending, and more than four in ten say they or a household member have used up all or most of their savings due to their health care debt. Many also report more profound consequences like skipping payment on other bills, delaying college, or buying a home, or changing their housing situation because of their debt. One in seven adults with health care debt say they have been denied care by a provider due to unpaid bills.

---

statistics/#:~:text=Average%20Student%20Loan%20Debt%20in%20the%20United%20States,private%20nonprofit%20four-year%20institutions%20took%20on%20education%20debt
[40] Source-Kaiser Family Foundation (KFF)Report-June 2022.

- <u>How does high indebtedness reduce economic growth or lead to economic stagnation?</u>

In three ways:

1. Reduces availability of funds for productive needs:

   As the demand for credit grows, there can be a "crowding out of credit" where productive investments can be cancelled, as funding might be used for other purposes. This can happen when Government and Corporate credit demand is high. The reduction of credit will slow economic activities.

2. Cost/benefit of funds:

   There is a point where the cost of borrowing exceeds its benefits. As there are a finite amount of financial resources, there is also a credit saturation point where the borrowers don't have any more borrowing capacity.

3. Unfavorable impact from a strong interest rate increase:

   One important risk refers to the impact of a strong increase in interest rates, it can cause a financial crisis. This happened as recently as 2007.

A strong increase in interest rates can have a strong unfavorable impact on debtors as they must pay more interest on servicing their loans. It affects all the borrowers (Governments, Corporations and Households) as well as investors who purchase that securitized debt. This reduces consumption which can generate an economic recession.

The impact can be worse if it becomes a financial crisis, due to lack of liquidity in the financial markets, or the insolvency of some important financial institutions, and because households lose wealth while their debt does not disappear. This scenario not only complicates economic recovery, but it runs the risk that the economy slows down so much, that it can enter a situation of secular (long-term) stagnation.

CHAPTER 5

ROAD MAP TO STRONGER ECONOMIC GROWTH

The roadmap to stronger economic growth includes the following recommendations:

A. Demand side recommendations to reduce income inequality.

B. Supply side recommendations to increase the economy's productive capacity in a non-inflationary manner through an increase of the labor force participation.

A. Reducing Income inequality

Background

According to an Organization for Economic Cooperation and Development (OECD) analysis, inequality reduces economic growth[41]. Reducing income inequality would boost economic growth. Their research found that countries where income inequality is decreasing grow faster than those with rising inequality.

The single biggest impact on growth is the widening gap between the lower middle class and poor households, compared to the rest of society.

In this respect, many social policies are aimed at poverty alleviation. However, it is not just poverty (i.e. the incomes of the lowest 10% of the population) that inhibits growth. Instead, their research suggests that policymakers need to be concerned about the bottom 40% more generally - including the vulnerable lower middle classes at risk of failing to benefit from the recovery and future growth. Anti-poverty programs will not be enough.

The other major set of policy insights from their research concerns the links between inequality and human capital.

---

[41] OECD Research, September 12, 2014.

The evidence strongly suggests that high inequality hinders the ability of individuals from low economic backgrounds to invest in their human capital, both in terms of the level of education but even more importantly in terms of the quality of education.

This requires that education policy focus on improving access by low-income groups, whose educational outcomes are not only worse on average from those of middle- and top-income groups, but also more sensitive to increases in inequality.

Government transfers have an important role to play in guaranteeing that low-income households do not fall further back in the income distribution. This is not only restricted to cash transfers. Other important elements of these policies promote and increase access to public services. This concerns services such as high-quality education or access to health services. Such measures smooth inequality stemming from cash incomes immediately, but they furthermore constitute a longer-term social investment to foster upward mobility and create greater equality of opportunities in the long run.

Accordingly, strategies to foster skills development must include improved job-related training and education for the low-skilled (on-the-job training) and better access to formal education over their working lives.

In the US educated workers have fared better; the wages received by those who finished their education with a four-year college degree grew from 134% of high school graduates' wages to 168%.

Finally, the OECD paper[42] also finds no evidence that redistributive policies, such as taxes and social benefits,

---

[42] Why Wages Aren't Growing in America by Jay Shambaugh and Ryan Nunn October 24, 2017 Harvard Business Review

harm economic growth, provided these policies are well designed, targeted, and implemented.

Compelling evidence proves that addressing high and growing inequality is critical to promote strong and sustained growth.

Therefore, in the US, to reduce income inequality and foster more economic growth, we prioritize our recommendations based on the important impact they have on most households. We begin with health care and then we continue with higher education.

Relative Importance of Various Items in the Expenditures of an Average U.S. Household (2022)

Item	Percent of Total Household Expenditures
Housing	40%
Transportation	19%
Food	14%
Medical Care	10%
Education	2%
Other	15%

Source: US Bureau of Labor Statistics.

During the past 20 years, health care and higher education have had the highest price increases in the economy. We feel that health care and higher education are key areas to address in seeking to correct income inequality in the US.

Two recommendations to help achieve the goal of income equality would be:
- Providing free public universal health care for those who request it.

- Providing a free public four-year college education and ending student debt.

We recommend free access to Public Health Services for those who want it. This would not eliminate the availability of Private Health Insurance for those who prefer it and are willing to pay for it.

This benefit has the greatest impact on the population, because:
1. The cost of health services and of health insurance is constantly increasing.
2. It absorbs an increasingly major share of a household's income.
3. It does not currently protect the total population.
4. Many households have difficulties dealing with their medical debt. This benefit is available in many countries.

Who has health insurance?

According to the U.S. Census Bureau. An estimated 304 million, or 92.1%, of Americans had health insurance at some point in 2022.

Private health insurance was more prevalent than public health insurance in 2022, with 65.6% of insured adults having a private healthcare plan compared to 36.1% having a public healthcare plan.

- Employment-based health insurance was the most common subtype of health insurance coverage, covering 54.5% of the American population.
- Medicaid and Medicare were the second most common subtype of health insurance in 2022, covering 18.8% and 18.7% of the population.
- Direct-purchase healthcare, such as Affordable Care Act (ACA) plans, covered 9.9% of the population,

- followed by TRICARE (2.4%), and VA and CHAMPVA coverage (1%).
- However, many Americans struggle to afford the cost of healthcare insurance. According to health insurance statistics from the Centers for Disease Control and Prevention, uninsured non-elderly adults (between ages 18 and 64) report that the top reason why they don't have health insurance is that the cost is too high[43].

Who doesn't have health insurance?

United States health insurance statistics show that Americans are worried about health insurance costs and being able to afford healthcare.

Cost is preventing people from getting care; 8.7% of adults reported not seeing a doctor in 2021 because of the expense.

- An estimated 26.6 million Americans didn't have health insurance at any point during 2022.
- The reasons uninsured nonelderly adults (between the ages 18 and 64) reported they don't have health insurance is that the cost is too high (69.6%); others because of eligibility issues; and others by not feeling they need to be insured.
- Nearly 25% of adults reported that either they or a member in their household has skipped doses of medicine, cut pills in half or not filled a prescription in the last year due to cost.
- About four in 10 adults (41%) reported having debt from unpaid medical or dental bills.
- Dental services are the most common type of healthcare that adults will delay due to costs (35%).

---

[43] US Census. September 12, 2023, **Written by** Katherine Keisler-Starkey, Lisa N. Bunch, and Rachel A. Lindstrom Report Number P60-281

That's followed by vision services (25%) and a doctor's visit (24%).
- Health insurance for young adults is lacking. Young adults have the highest uninsured percentages of any age group with 14% of people 19 to 25 without health insurance and 12.5% of people 26 to 34 without coverage in 2022.
- Hispanic adults had the largest uninsured percentage (23.4%), followed by Black adults at 11.4%. Meanwhile, 7.4% of Asian adults and 6.8% of non-Hispanic White adults didn't have health insurance in 2022.

Health care expenses

According to the American Public Health Association (2022) The United States spends the most by far on health care among all 36 countries in the Organization for Economic Co-operation and Development (OECD).

- Total National Healthcare Expenditures (NHE) in the US reached $4.5 trillion in 2022. The average family of four in the US in 2020 spent about $25,000 in health insurance (premiums and deductibles).
- The pricing system is inherently the single greatest driver of health care costs. The rising total National Health Expenses (NHE) are primarily driven by private health care insurers and pharmaceutical expenditures.
- Private insurers drive the largest segment of excess cost in the U.S. health care system. Since health care expenses are not proportional to personal income, individuals with low incomes pay a larger percentage of their household income toward health care costs. Thus, the private health insurance market exacerbates wealth inequality by functioning in a manner like a regressive tax.

- Drug prices are significantly higher in the United States than in any other OECD country. Prescription drug expenditures alone will represent 19.7% of the U.S. GDP by 2028. Increased prescription drug expenditures will be largely driven by manufacturers' increases in drug prices. One of the distinctions in U.S. prescription policy is the burden of drug costs borne by patients as out-of-pocket costs.

- Those with low incomes faced financial hardship or were unable to pay their medical bills, resulting in food insecurity and inability to take prescribed medications. Even among the insured, close to 40% of patients with insurance still faced financial hardship due to the out-of-pocket expenses associated with their plans. One study revealed that high-deductible plans led to delays in diagnosis and treatment of breast cancer in women. Despite the passage of the Affordable Care Act (ACA), there are also persistent racial health disparities in the U.S. uninsured population.

Cost of health insurance

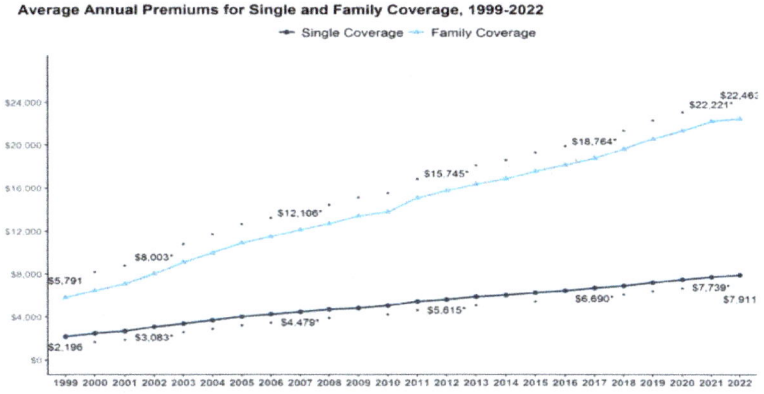

Source: KFF Employer Health Benefits Survey, 2022

- In 2020 the average annual single premium per enrolled employee for employer-based health insurance is $7,590/year in the U.S., with employees contributing $1,637 and employers contributing $5,953 annually.

- The average annual deductible per enrolled employee in employer-based health insurance is $3,811/year for families and $1,992/year for single coverage.

- An average premium increase of 6% is expected among ACA health insurance marketplace insurers in 2024, according to KFF. Those higher costs not only put a strain on individuals but can also hurt small businesses.

Providing free public four-year college education and ending student debt

We recommend:
1. Extending higher public education to cover at least four years of free college education,
2. End future Student Educational Debt.
3. Restructure total existing debt balance to be completely paid-off by 2040.

In our previous books, we have recommended an Educational Reform that will provide all students with the option of four years of free public College or Vocational education. This recommendation does not exclude the option for students to choose instead to attend Private Universities, at their expense.

With respect to the existing debt, borrowers and lenders should negotiate a fair amortization plan that might take into consideration their income levels, government subsidies and debt reduction. The main objective is to eliminate student debt in a fair manner and not let it occur again.
Why?

Because of the high cost of college education and its impact on increasing student debt.

Increasing costs[44]

The average cost of attending a four-year college or university in the United States rose by 497% between the 1985-86 and 2017-18 academic years, more than twice the rate of inflation.

In 1980, the price to attend a four-year college full-time was $10,231 annually—including tuition, fees, room, and board, and adjusted for inflation—according to the National Center for Education Statistics. By 2019-20, the total price increased to $28,775. That's a 180% increase.

College prices have soared across all institution types, even private nonprofit institutions continue to cost more than public colleges. A full-time student paid $48,965 at a private nonprofit college on average in 2019-20 compared to $21,035 at a public university.[45]

Important problem - reductions in state and local funding

Aside from tuition payments, public institutions depend on funding from states and localities to operate. State and local funding made up 55% of public two-year college revenues and 44% of public four-year college revenues in 2018-19, according to the College Board.

The amount states and local governments give to colleges fluctuates depending on market conditions and tax revenues. Economic downturns like the Great Recession in

---

[44] *College Tuition Is Rising at Twice the Inflation Rate—While Students Learn at Home-Forbes 08/2020 *by Erik Sherman*

[45] College Tuition Inflation: Compare The Cost of College Over Time Brianna McGurran -Alicia Hahn- Updated: May 9, 2023,

2008 led to funding cuts, and in 2020, average education appropriations per full-time equivalent student were still 6% lower overall than in 2008, according to a report from the State Higher Education Executive Officers Association (SHEEO).

When public colleges have less state and local funding, it's more likely they'll pass costs on to students in the form of tuition increases, according to a 2019 report from the Center on Budget and Policy Priorities.

State and local funding per student for higher education dropped about 25% between 1988 and 2018, according to an analysis by Douglas A. Webber, an associate professor of economics at Temple University.

The impact - Increasing student debt

Average federal student loan debt: the majority of student loan debt in the U.S. is made up of federal student loans. The total federal loan portfolio is more than $1.7 trillion. This is spread amongst nearly 44 million borrowers, according to Federal Student Aid.

In 2023 the total student debt reached a balance of $1.7 trillion dollars, owed by 43.6 million borrowers. After mortgages, student debt is the second highest consumer debt category.

From an economic point of view, the high debt servicing of those loans reduces the borrowers' purchasing power and therefore lowers their consumption, which impacts the economy by slowing growth.

Our recommendation will help people get educated so they can improve their careers and stop their indebtedness. The goal is to provide everyone accessibility to higher education so they can improve their income.

This will not eliminate the option of private college education for those that can afford it or qualify for their financial aid.

<u>It can be done.</u>

An important example of what can be done in the meantime, was published December 8 of 2023 in the Washington Post, about the University of Virginia (UV) where the university bolstered its financial aid plan for its students.

UV is ranked as one of the top public universities in the US. The annual cost of tuition is about $40,000 for in-state students and about $80,000 for out-of-state students.

Their student financial aid program provides grants and scholarships that cover the full cost of tuition and fees for in-state students from families that made $80,000 or less.

Now the income threshold has increased to $100,000 or less and families that earn an income of $50,000 or less will receive full financial aid covering tuition, fees, meals, and housing.

B. Increasing the Economy's Productive Capacity

<u>Increasing labor force participation.</u>

We recommend the payment by the Federal Government of day-care for full-time female and single parent workers. This measure will increase the labor force and generate more income and tax revenues which will contribute towards the growth of the economy.
This is necessary because as the economy and the population continue to grow, there will be an increased demand for goods and services.

Among the options to increase the increased demand for goods and services is by importing them from abroad.

Unfortunately, this option has a negative impact on the rate of economic growth.

Another way is by increasing the amount of capital and labor or by reaching a higher productivity level. Experts consider that increasing the labor force can be a more favorable option. Is it feasible?

To increase the labor force given the demographic trends, a study by the Brookings Institution compared different flows of immigration to the US and their impact on the size of the total population. In all instances they could partially increase the size of the labor force. This will help but will be subject to multiple caveats among others, the shrinking size of the global population.

Therefore, presently we feel that the most immediate solution with the current population is through women that are not part of the labor force because of the high cost of day care. Reversing the drop of women's participation in the labor force will be a win-win situation for everyone.

This measure will increase the labor force and generate more income and tax revenues which will contribute towards the growth of the economy.

Labor force participation

Labor force participation varies by marital status and differs between women and men.

Across all marital statuses, men were more likely to participate in the labor force than their female counterparts. Married men were more likely to participate in the labor force (71.4 percent) than separated men (69.8 percent), never-married men (66.3 percent), and divorced men (63.6 percent). Labor force participation rates for widowed women and men, who tend to be older, were 17.9 percent and 23.3 percent, respectively.[46]

LABOR FORCE PARTICIPATION IN THE US 1950 - 2050

Labor Force Participation Rates	Men	Women
1950	86.4	33.9
1960	83.3	37.7
1970	79.7	43.3
1980	77.4	51.5
1990	76.4	57.5
2000	74.8	59.9
2005	73.3	59.3
2010	72.6	59.7
2020	70.0	59.4
2030	67.4	56.5
2040	66.5	55.5
2050	66.0	55.1

Source: US Department of Labor

The rapid rise in women's labor force participation was a major development in the labor market during the second half of the 20th century. Overall, women's labor force participation increased dramatically from the 1960s through the 1980s, before slowing in the 1990s and early 2000s.

Labor force participation among women then began a decline that accelerated in the period of the December 2007– June 2009 recession, hitting a pre-pandemic low in 2015 at 56.7 percent. The rate then rose to 57.4 percent in

---

[46] Bureau of Labor Statistics, https://www.bls.gov/emp/tables/civilian-labor-force-participation-rate.htm

2019, before the pandemic affected the labor market. Women's labor force participation rate was 56.2 percent in 2020.[47]

Never-married women had the highest participation rate of all women, at 63.5 percent in 2020. Separated and divorced women were more likely to participate in the labor force (61.7 percent and 59.7 percent, respectively) than married women (57.4 percent).

Unmarried mothers are much more likely to participate in the labor force than married mothers. In March 2020, 77.7 percent of unmarried mothers were in the labor force, compared with 70.4 percent of married mothers.

The labor force participation rate for women with children under 18 years of age was 72.5 percent in March 2020, much lower than the rate of 93.1 percent for men with children under 18 years. Among mothers, the labor force participation rate for those with children 6 to 17 years old, at 76.4 percent, was considerably higher than for those with younger children. The rate for women with children under 6 years old was 67.4 percent, and the rate for women with children under 3 years old was 65.6 percent.

By comparison, the labor force participation rate for men was 67.7 percent in 2020, down by 1.5 percentage points from the previous year and the lowest rate in the history of the series. The steep declines in 2020 reflect the impact of the COVID-19 pandemic on the labor market.

The labor force participation rate for fathers was similar regardless of the age of their children; the rate was 92.0 percent for fathers with children 6 to 17 years old, 94.5 percent for fathers of children under 6 years old, and 94.7 percent for fathers of children under 3 years old.

---

[47] Women in the labor force: a Databook-BLS Reports (1097- March 2022).

Researchers (London School of Economics) examined family policy across high-income Western European countries, Canada and the US and found that investments in childcare and early childhood learning had significant impacts on women's labor force participation.

Conclusion:

All the proposed programs (public healthcare, free public four-year college education and payment of daycare) will generate significant financial requirements as the Federal Government will have to finance them in an environment of high and risky volumes of indebtedness.

In the next chapter we discuss how to address these challenges.

CHAPTER 6

FINANCIAL CHALLENGES
AND
NEEDED REFORMS

To implement the recommended measures and programs, important financial measures and reforms will have to be taken.

We will begin with the public sector as it will have increasing demands that require a healthy financial situation, which currently is not the case as the Federal Government operates with strong deficits and has reached a very high level of debt.

Second, the risk of increased financial fragility of the economy must be addressed as the level of debt continues to increase through private corporations that are incurring heavy debts and are doing so by operating increasingly with the "Shadow Banks", many of which operate in a risky and unregulated manner.

A. Addressing Public Sector Challenges

CHALLENGES

Increasing US federal deficits

In May of 2023 the Congressional Budget Office (CBO) presented their long-term Federal budget projection. In this report they estimate increasing deficits from 5.3% of Gross Domestic Product (GDP) in 2023, to 10.0% of GDP by 2053, as Federal Expenses continue to exceed revenues. These estimates do not include the additional expenses the Federal Government should assume proposed in this book, which could worsen the deficit estimates.

In CBO's projections, net interest outlays and healthcare programs will be the major contributors for the growth of total deficits.

Public debt

By the end of 2023 CBO estimates the Federal Debt will equal 123% of GDP and by 2053 it will grow to 181% of GDP. Such a level of debt will slow economic growth, push up interest payments and will limit further borrowing for any emergency or priority needs.

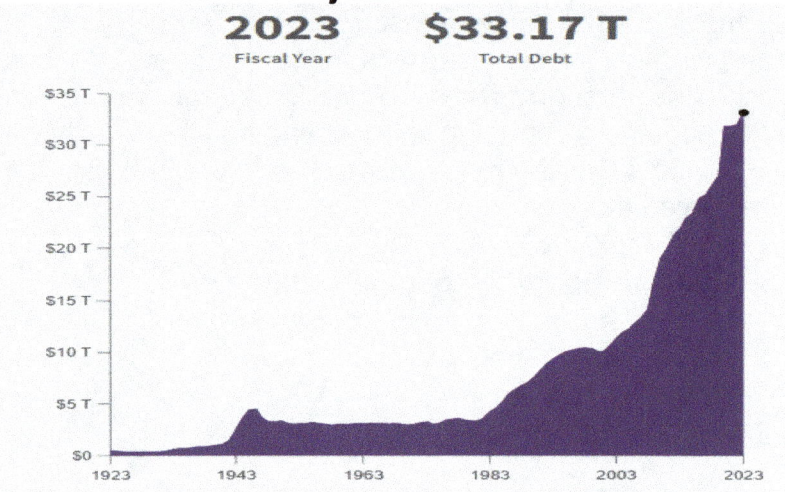

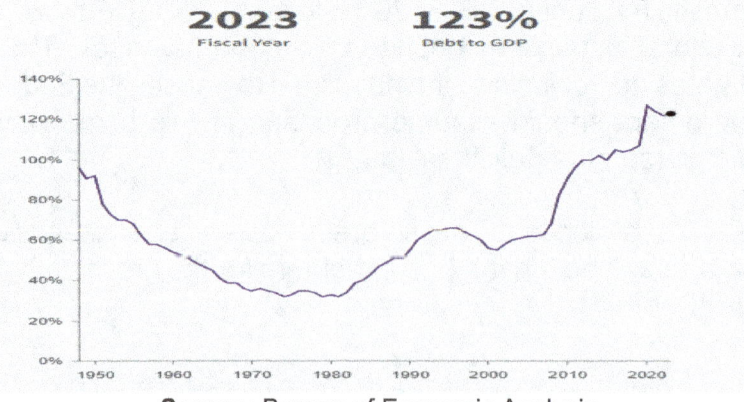

Source: Bureau of Economic Analysis

Unless important reforms are adopted to reduce the public debt, there will be important financial constraints to address an increased demand for more entitlements.

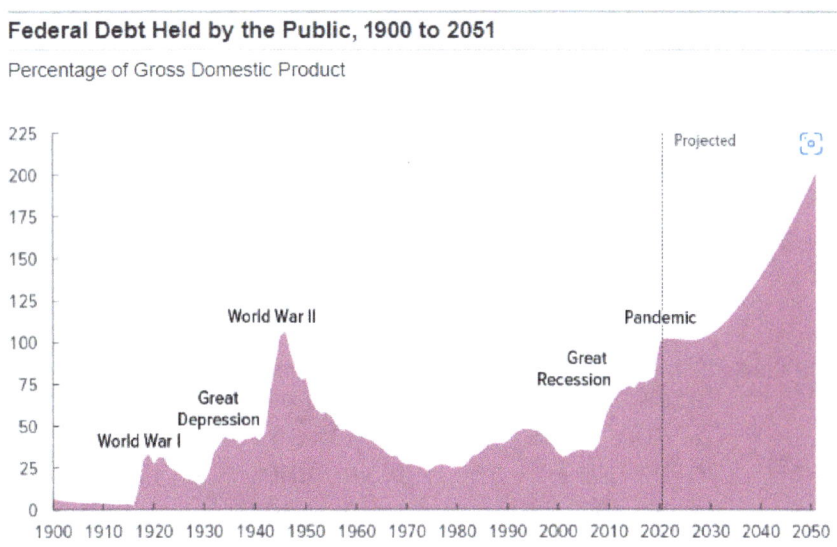

Federal Debt Held by the Public, 1900 to 2051
Percentage of Gross Domestic Product

RECOMMENDATIONS

Implement a fiscal reform

To finance the needs for more entitlements and seek to reduce/eliminate the public debt, we propose a fiscal reform that will increase revenues and match expenses to the increasing social needs. What must be done?

a. Addressing Current Federal Budget Expenses:

Government spending is broken down into three categories:
- mandatory spending
- discretionary spending
- interest on the national debt

Each category of spending has different subcategories.

Mandatory expenditures, such as Social Security, Medicare, and the Supplemental Nutrition Assistance Program, accounted for about 65% of the budget in 2022. These must be prioritized.

1. Addressing mandatory expenses

Social Security

The Social Security program is funded by dedicated tax revenues; the balance is collected from income taxes on Social Security Benefits. Revenues from the payroll tax and the income tax on benefits are credited to the Old-Age and Survivors Insurance (OASI) Trust Fund and the Disability Insurance (DI) Trust Fund, which finance the program's benefits. CBO projects the OASI trust fund will be exhausted in 2033 and the DI trust fund by 2048.

Currently the Social Security System is running a sizable deficit, which is projected to rise if no changes are made. The fund will reach its exhaustion by 2035, which means the payroll tax receipts will be able to finance about 80% of the benefits it provides.

If the outlays were to match its revenues, benefits would have to be reduced by about 25% in 2034 and up to 30% by 2052.

It must be noted that tax revenues for both trust funds will decrease from 4.5% of GDP in 2022, to 4.4% in 2052. The reasons for the shortages are mainly due to a shortfall of revenues as the amount of earned income subject to Social Security tax has fallen to 82.5% from the 90% it was four decades ago, because of the greater income inequality where earned income of higher income people has increased much more rapidly than the income of lower income people.

Currently the maximum amount of earned income on which social security tax is collected (and from where the benefits are determined) is $160,200 a year, adjusted annually for inflation.

As more people will be retiring some of the options being proposed to improve the solvency of the program include the following:

Changes in benefits:
- Limiting Benefit growth (this is one of the most impactful)
- Gradually raising the retirement age

Changes in revenues:
- Make investment income subject to social security taxation
- Raising the cap of maximum taxable earned income.
- Increase the payroll tax rate.
- Cover newly hired state and local workers

Medicare

With respect to health care programs, expenditures have consistently grown faster than the economy, as health care costs per person continue to increase (this represents two thirds of the future increases), as well as to the aging of the population (equivalent to one third of the future increases).

In 2022 federal spending on the major health care programs was 5.8% of GDP and is expected to increase to 8.8% by 2052. These programs benefited over 65 million people by the end of Fiscal 2022. This represented over 11% of total Federal expenses. By 2028, the Medicare Trust Fund, which pays for hospitals, skilled nursing facilities and hospices is expected to be exhausted.

President Biden proposed in his 2024 Budget adding more drugs to the list for price negotiations to reduce expenses and raising the Medicare tax rate on earned and unearned income of people who earn more than $400,000 a year, increasing their tax rate from 3.8% to 5%, to increase revenues. The tax increase will include more pass-through firms.

The WAPO proposed additional actions to stabilize Medicare finances. To reduce costs, among other options, it recommends:
- containing costs for Medicare Advantage
- adopting "site-neutral "payments

Additionally, from the Brookings Institution, L. Adler and B. Ippolito in March of 2023 proposed a pro-competitive health care reform that seeks to reduce costs by enhancing more competition in the health care sector.

2. Where to cut discretionary expenses

An editorial from the Washington Post (07/12/2023) proposed 'a smarter federal budget" meaning that they found evidence that the federal government can perform its functions at a lower cost. They cited examples of refocused spending on weapons systems in all branches of the armed services, as well as a more economic Medicare reimbursement rate for outpatient services and the need for farm subsidies.

b. Increasing Revenues

1. Tax revenues

Work of the Organization for Economic Cooperation and Development (OECD) has focused on top incomes to reduce inequality through reforms to tax and benefit policies.

They recommend governments re-examine their tax systems to ensure that wealthier individuals contribute their fair share of the tax burden. This aim can be achieved in several different ways – not only via raising marginal tax rates on the rich but also improving tax compliance, eliminating, or scaling back tax deductions which tend to benefit high earners disproportionally, and reassessing the role of taxes on all forms of property and wealth, including the transfer of assets. Broadening the tax base by closing loopholes in the current tax code has the potential to raise both efficiency and equity.

These are some examples of solutions recommended by experts. The adoption of these or other better reforms are key to the future welfare of the country.

- The WAPO proposed increasing the corporate rate from 21% to 25%.

- The Brookings Institution (W. Gale & S. Vignaux-Sept. 7,2023) propose the following changes:
    - Capital Gains reform
    - Taxing intergenerational wealth transfers
    - Eliminating the Section 199A deduction for qualified business incomes
    - Creating a Value Added Tax (VAT)

Most of these measures are geared mainly to the wealthy without harming economic growth, while helping to reduce income inequality.

2. Additional option to increase revenues

A different innovative alternative that can help increase revenues for the Federal Government could be through the establishment of minority business partnerships between the government (with a 10-20% participation) and private companies that benefit from federal contracts to produce goods and services that:
- don't have competition
- have shortages
- are strategic for the nation's security
- and/or with Organizations, Corporations, Farms that benefit from government subsidies

The revenues would go to a trust fund which would invest them and use them if needed only for mandatory expenses.

In addition to the reforms needed in the public sector, given the elevated amounts of debt of the private sector and the way it operates, it also must go through some important reforms that will prevent the occurrence of a severe financial crisis.

B. Addressing Private Sector challenges

CHALLENGES

US credit expansion

The total US corporate debt was $22.5 trillion[48] in 2022. For comparison, it was $8.97 trillion in 2006.

---

[48] Statista

These numbers include both non-financial and financial corporations, with the latter responsible for about a third.

US corporations issued an immense amount of debt in 2020 to make up for the adverse effects of the pandemic. The trend continued in 2021, but there is an important distinction to be made. Companies issued further debt in 2021 not simply because of unsatisfactory revenues, but also to push back maturities. In other words, they were delaying the inevitable and thus making it likely that in a few years' time, by 2025, the total nonfinancial debt to mature could reach $968.5 billion, compared to $570 billion in 2022.

This debt includes all outstanding debt securities, that is, bonds plus debentures, notes, and deposits, but not direct loans. American companies presently owe more than $10.5 trillion just in bonds. Prior to the pandemic, outstanding bonds were $8.8 trillion.[49]

US corporate debt rating[50]

Debt is usually classified as either investment grade or speculative grade. The former is very much preferable and generally considered lower risk.

Speculative debt is often held by companies of poor credit rating and, as such, has a higher likelihood of default. Junk-rated (high yield) bonds are an example of this risk in corporate bonds. At present, 28% of corporate debt across both financial and non-financial corporations in the US is speculative.

---

[49] Worrisome US Corporate Debt Statistics for 2023-Written by Jordan T. Prodanoff Updated · May 20, 2023
[50] Statista

RECOMMENDATIONS

Reducing the risks of increasing corporate debt

To address corporate debt, in our book "*The Era of Two Speeds*" we made some recommendations that will not stop lending but rather make it more controllable, to avoid the type of lending that generates "Financial Bubbles" or other risky operations that the "Shadow Banking" institutions do, in an un-supervised manner.

In that book we included reference to The Financial System Stability Assessment Report from the International Monetary Fund (IMF) in 2020 that provided an ample number of measures geared to strengthen the US financial system.

These proposed measures are not geared to stop lending activities, rather they seek to:
- Reduce the federal deficit and debt to provide a greater financial capacity for other priorities.
- Regulate the lending activities of Shadow Banks to corporations, to diminish the financial fragility risk.

CHAPTER 7

EPILOGUE

By 2050 the American economy should continue to be amongst the largest and strongest in the world. That will be the result of the continued presence of those factors that make it what it is presently.

Nevertheless, during the following decades, because of the demographic trends of slower population growth and greater population aging, the economy will be facing strong pressures towards its growth deceleration.

Some favorable trends, such as the flow of immigrants and technological improvements will help in moderating the growth deceleration. But the slowing down of the economy will be a generalized phenomenon affecting most of the economies in the world, as many countries like China, Korea and some European nations are already being impacted by their demographic trends.

About the potential risk of the economy entering a state of economic stagnation, this risk is based on the high and increasing level of indebtedness of the government, the Corporations and even the households. This, as we have previously explained, makes the economy vulnerable to a strong price shock, because of its financial fragility.

If a financial crisis were to occur, it might be very difficult to overcome it because of the high levels of indebtedness, which would limit the capacity to respond, therefore potentially causing the economy to enter a state of secular stagnation.

To address the current and future challenges, our recommendations seek mainly three objectives:

- Increase the rate of economic growth through actions that will improve most of the population's income and its purchasing power, as this will have a strong impact

on consumption, the largest component of the aggregate demand.
- Improve the populations potential to achieve their "American Dream".
- Reduce the financial fragility of the economy through important actions in the Public and Private sectors.

This will not only strengthen the economy but will also make the "American Dream" achievable again.

Strengthening the Capitalist Economy

The increase of funds directed to pay for pensions, Medicare, higher education, and daycare benefits would seem like a trend towards the socialization of the economy, where the State becomes the paternal benefactor. Ironically, the recommended actions are necessary to support the strengthening of the capitalist economy.

If the economy stagnates or shrinks, not only more government expenses would be necessary, and even then, many private sector companies would perish.

The role of the government must be very effective in supporting the population to keep the economy strong and growing. For this the Fiscal Reform plays an important role to make the government more efficient and effective and less dependent on increased public debt. By reducing or preferably eliminating the Public Debt, the increasing amount of revenues destined for debt servicing, can instead be used to address the increasing mandatory expenses.

By doing this, government actions will increase investment; will increase workers purchasing power; will increase the number of Jobs; will even increase its fiscal revenues, so that the economy evolves on a solvent and sustainable manner.

Necessary Political Changes

To implement many important policies, such as the reduction of public expenditures or the increase of taxes, will require realistically that public officials particularly in the legislatures adopt those measures without the pressure of lobbyists or interest groups that finance their electoral campaigns. For that purpose, a new public expense burden, but limited in its level, should finance their electoral campaigns, and prohibit the use of private funds for those purposes.

This recommendation is intended to facilitate the important decisions that must be taken for the benefit of the nation, giving legislators complete autonomy to do their work without the pressures of groups and individuals self-interest.

In his book "The Price of Inequality" written by Nobel Prize winner in Economics, Joseph E Stiglitz, paraphrasing what he said: he proposed a significant number of reforms that will not eliminate inequality, but rather just reduce the level of inequality. This is because while the market forces play some role in the creation of the level of inequality; the market forces are ultimately shaped by politics.

So, he asks, "The question, is can we get there?"

He believes that reform can happen when the wealthiest and most powerful realize that the impact of less income inequality, that is, greater economic growth, benefits their own interest.

TECHNICAL APPENDIX

- ❖ Economic Growth
- ❖ Income Inequality
- ❖ Financial Fragility

ABOUT ECONOMIC GROWTH

What the US economy must address now and particularly in the future is how to maintain and or generate strong economic growth, not only for the benefit of the population, but because it is fundamental to support the additional requirements resulting from the population and economic trends.

Different components determine the long-term growth of the economy and the short-term growth of the economy.

In the short-term growth is determined by the behavior of the Aggregate Demand?

What Is Aggregate Demand?

Aggregate demand is a measurement of the total amount of demand for all finished goods and services produced in an economy. Aggregate demand is commonly expressed as the total amount of money exchanged for those goods and services at a specific price level and point in time.

Aggregate Demand Components

Aggregate demand is determined by the overall collective spending on products and services by all economic sectors on the procurement of goods and services in four distinct components:

<u>Consumption Spending (C)</u>

Consumption spending (C) is the largest component of an economy's aggregate demand. In the American economy it represents about 70% of the aggregate demand.
Consumption refers to the total spending of individuals and households on goods and services in the economy. Consumption spending does not include spending on

residential structures, which is accounted for in the investment spending component.

Consumption spending depends on several factors, such as disposable income, debt, consumer expectations of future economic conditions, taxes, and interest rates.

Investment Spending (I)

Investment spending (I) is the total expenditure on new capital goods and services such as machinery, equipment, changes in inventories, investments in nonresidential structures, and residential structures.

In the US, Gross Investment represents 18.5-20.0% of the aggregate demand.

Investment spending depends on factors such as interest rates, future expectations regarding the economy, and government incentives.

Government Spending (G)

Government spending (G) is the total amount of expenditure by the government on infrastructure, investments, defense and military equipment, public sector facilities, healthcare services, and government employees.

It excludes the spending on transfer payments, such as pension plans, Medicare, subsidies, and aid transfers to other countries.

The government expenditures in the American economy represent 15.5% of the aggregate demand.

Net Exports (X–M)

Exports are products that are produced by domestic producers and sold abroad, while imports are products that are manufactured abroad and imported for domestic purchase.

It is important to remember that aggregate demand is the total demand for **domestically** produced goods and services; therefore, exports are added to the aggregate demand, whereas imports are subtracted.

The measure of exports minus imports is called Net Exports, an important determinant of aggregate demand.

ABOUT INCOME INEQUALITY

National Income Shares

The following was copied and edited from OECD February 2015 Report.

National income is the sum of all income available to the residents of a given country in a given year.

The division of total national income shared between the factors of production, labor, and capital, is called the functional distribution of income. The labor income share (or labor share) is the part of national income allocated to labor compensation, while the capital share is the part of national income going to the capitalist.

Labor Income Share

The labor income share is calculated as the compensation of employees over total economy GDP multiplied by total employment.

Since the late 1970s, large wage gains have accrued to workers at the top of the distribution, and wages have been declining or stagnant for the bottom half of the income distribution.

Labor's share of income has fallen from nearly 65% in the mid-1970s to below 57% in 2017. As the share of income channeled to labor has declined, the distribution of income has become more unequal.

In recent years, a growing body of evidence suggests that labor shares have seen a secular downward trend with important negative consequences. Data shows that trends in labor shares negatively affect the main macroeconomic aggregates, namely household consumption, private sector investment, net exports and government consumption.

What caused the falling of labor's income share?

The usual explanations for changes in labor shares include technological change, globalization, financial markets, product and labor market institutions, the bargaining power of labor and unemployment.

Technological changes are often presented as the main culprit, with some authors seeing the role of capital accumulation and capital-augmenting technical change as determinants of the evolution of the labor share.

According to OECD estimates (OECD, 2012), total factor productivity (TFP) growth and capital deepening – the key drivers of economic growth – accounted for most of the average within-industry decline of the labor share in OECD countries between 1990 and 2007.

Another possibility is that trends in the labor share are determined by a shift in employment from labor-intensive to more capital-intensive sectors, where labor shares are lower. An ILO study also found that the shift in sectoral composition was indeed a contributory factor in many countries, but that in advanced economies most of the fall in the labor share was the result of falling shares within industries (ILO, 2010).

Indeed, the labor share is significantly different across industries. This decline is widespread across industries, since essentially all industries experienced a considerable decline of the labor share in the last 20 years.

A key question, therefore, is whether the decline of the aggregate labor share has been the result of a structural shift away from labor-intensive activities or whether instead it has been the result of a decline in the labor share within each industry.

The ILO (2011) found falling labor shares for low- and medium-skilled workers but increasing shares for highly skilled workers in a sample of ten developed economies.

Studies typically also find smaller negative effects of globalization on the labor share in high-income countries. It is possible that redistribution from labor to capital has occurred through offshoring.

The role of financial markets has also been highlighted, particularly its influence on businesses to increase shareholder value and to focus on their core activities while subcontracting labor-intensive activities.

Of particular attention have been factors such as union density, minimum wage legislation, unemployment benefits and coverage, severance pay and government consumption. The decline in union density – the number of trade union members as a percentage of total employees or as a percentage of total employment – in many developed economies has often been linked to the weakening of workers' bargaining power, negatively affecting their ability to negotiate a larger share of productivity growth as labor compensation.

The level of the minimum wage and other "intermediary" institutions, including employment protection legislation, the generosity of unemployment benefit and other benefits and contributions (the 'tax wedge'), are among the institutional variables that have been widely used in empirical studies.

High unemployment can place downward pressure on wage demands and on the labor share, while the level of unemployment benefits can have an impact on the labor share by affecting workers' "reservation wages", that is, the level of pay workers would accept as a minimum.

The effects of declining labor shares

Over time and across many countries, a higher capital share is associated with higher inequality in the personal distribution of income (Piketty 2013).

It is important to note that, when the negative impacts of falling labor share on private consumption are not offset by investment, countries tend to rely more on credit (household debts) and/or net exports to maintain aggregate demand. This may contribute to increasing economic instability and global imbalances.

If many countries simultaneously pursue policies of wage moderation (as defined by wage growth lower than labor productivity growth), the result is likely to be a shortfall in global aggregate demand, with negative effects on most countries.

The positive effect on consumption of redistribution from the capital to the labor share has been attributed to the fact that the propensity to consume out of labor compensation is higher than the propensity to consume out of capital income, as the labor share goes to households with lower incomes and therefore able to save lower proportions of their income than wealthier people, who save a higher proportion of their total incomes.

Income Inequality.[51]

The following are the key takeaways from Melissa Schettini's of Brookings Institution in her testimony before the Congressional Joint Economic Committee:

1. The chances of moving from bottom to top income quintile are lower in the U.S. than in other nations.

2. There is a very strong relationship between the incomes of parents and the incomes their children will have as adults. Inequality, in other words, is strongly inherited.

3. Rates of relative intergenerational mobility in the U.S. appear to have been flat for decades.

4. It is a different story, however, for absolute mobility – which indicates how well a person does compared to their parents in absolute terms, rather than relative ones. On this measure of mobility, most Americans born in 1940 ended up better off, while those born a few decades later have seen a sharp decline compared to their parents at the same age. Only half of those of those born in 1980 have surpassed their parent's family income.

5. Place matters for mobility. There are too, right down to the county and city level. Cities in the Deep South and Midwest tend to have more sluggish mobility than other regions. In this sense, the American Dream persists – it is just unevenly distributed.

6. There is a gender gap in terms of the impact of place. Boys who grow up in low-opportunity places feel the

---

[51] Melissa Schettini Kearney, Testimony before the Joint Economic Committee "Income Inequality in the United States", January 16, 2014

effects much more strongly than girls. Growing up in Baltimore City, for example, reduces boys' household income by 27.9 percent.[52]

7. Education helps to boost outcomes, starting at the pre-K level. An experienced kindergarten teacher boosts earnings by $1,104 on average.

8. A college education acts as a leveler. This is true for elite colleges, other four-year institutions, and community college.

9. The chances of going to college soon after high school are very strongly related to household income.

10. Being poor has implications for how long we are likely to live. In this sense, it is not an exaggeration to say that inequality is a matter of life and death. Again, the effect is most pronounced for men. Poverty takes nearly 10 years off their lifespan (from the age of 40).

---

[52] (https://www.brookings.edu/blog/social-mobility-memos/2015/06/19/boysto-men-fathers-family-and-opportunity/).

Fading of the American Dream

Contrary to popular belief, equality of opportunity in the U.S. is lower than in most advanced countries—and it is declining. A 2017 report by economist Raj Chetty and others indicates that an American born in 1940 was almost certain to become more prosperous than his or her parents. Someone born in 1980 is just as likely to be worse off, however. Declining equality of opportunity stems in large part from the high cost of higher education, coupled with spiraling economic inequality. Statistics from the World Inequality Database show that since about 1970 the income of the top 1 percent, corrected for inflation, has quadrupled, whereas that of the bottom 90 percent has stagnated. Men with only high school degrees have seen their incomes drop.

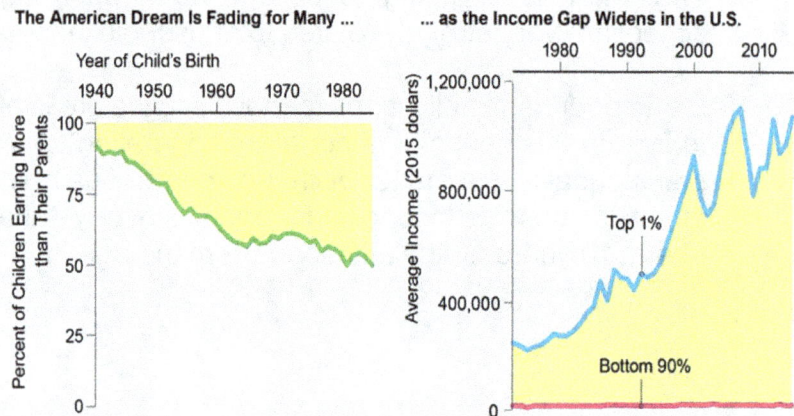

Source: Robert Reich, Saving Capitalism, Knopf Doubleday Publishing Group, September 29, 2015. Soaring wealth and income inequality are probably the main fuel for the belief that the American dream is dying.

ABOUT FINANCIAL FRAGILITY OF THE ECONOMY

Refers to the vulnerability of the economy to having a financial crisis, resulting from a shock, such as a relevant change in the cost of money (an increase in the interest rates and/or a devaluation of the foreign exchange rate).

There are basically three different levels of fragility:
- Low
- Moderate
- High

These levels are determined by the number of financial resources concentrated on a financial operation and the level of impact a price shock could have on the economy.

The greater the number of financial resources operated on a particular type of financial activity, the greater the potential risk, but the fragility level is determined by the impact that a price shock would have on it.

Securitization

The US financial system underwent a far-reaching transformation in the 1980s with the takeoff of securitization in the residential mortgage market.

Until the early 1980s, banks and savings institutions, like regional savings and loans, had been the dominant holders of home mortgages. Since then, Government-Sponsored Enterprises (GSEs) such as Fannie Mae and Freddie Mac became the dominant holders of home mortgages. This was done through the securitization of mortgages.

Securitization represents another type of financial innovation which expanded rapidly in the US over the past several decades. Securitization is the process of taking assets with cash flows, such as mortgages held by banks, and turning them into tradable securities (bonds).

With the emergence of securitization, banks sold their mortgage assets to institutions that financed these purchases by issuing mortgage-backed securities (MBSs).[53] Mortgage-backed bonds are the most familiar form of securitization, but the same basic process can be done with almost any kind of cash flow, including auto loans, college loans, credit card debt, business receivables.

The "shadow banking system" in the US is linked to the process of securitization, the expansion of asset-backed securities, including Collateralized Debt Obligations (CDOs), and the emergence of money market funds[54].

Market-based holdings now constitute two-thirds of the total of home mortgages. While residential mortgages have been the most important element in the evolution of securitization, the trend extends as well to other forms of lending, including consumer loans such as those for credit card and automobile purchases, and commercial real estate or corporate loans.[55]

Shadow Banking

The term "shadow bank" was coined by economist Paul McCulley in a 2007 speech at the annual financial symposium hosted by the Kansas City Federal Reserve Bank in Jackson Hole, Wyoming. In McCulley's talk, shadow

---

[53] John J. McConnell and Stephen A. Buser, The Origins and Evolution of the Market for Mortgage-Backed Securities, The Annual Review of Financial Economics, Annu. Rev. Finance. Econ. 2011. 3:173-92

[54] Zoltan Pozsar, The Rise and Fall of the Shadow Banking System, https://www.economy.com/sbs

[55] Robert Pollin & James Heintz, 2013. "Study of U.S. Financial System," FESSUD studies fstudy10, Financialization, Economy, Society & Sustainable Development (FESSUD) Project.

banking referred mainly to nonbank financial institutions that engaged in maturity transformation.

The term "shadow banking" describes a large segment of financial intermediation that is routed outside the balance sheets of regulated commercial banks and other depository institutions. Shadow banks are defined as financial intermediaries that conduct functions of banking "without access to central bank liquidity or public sector credit guarantees."[56]

The shadow banking system decomposes credit intermediation into a chain of wholesale-funded, securitization-based lending.

- Credit transformation: Enhancement of the credit quality of debt issued by the intermediary using priority of claims, use of third-party liquidity and credit put options as guarantees.
- Maturity Transformation: The use of short-term deposits to fund long term loans.
- Liquidity transformation: The use of liquid instruments to fund illiquid assets.

In the shadow banking system credit is intermediated through a wide range of securitization and secured funding techniques, including Asset-Backed Commercial Paper (ABCP), Asset-Backed Securities (ABS), Collateralized Debt Obligations (CDOs), Money Market Funds (MMF) and repurchase agreements (repos).

Other examples of shadow-banking activities include structured investment vehicles (highly leveraged investment funds which finance the purchase of long-term securities that

---

[56] Zoltan Pozsar, The Rise and Fall of the Shadow Banking System, https://www.economy.com/sbs

pay higher returns by issuing short-term securities), hedge funds which extend credit, and money market mutual funds.

Examples of shadow banks:
- Investment Banks
- Finance Companies
- Asset Backed Commercial Paper (ABCP) conduits.
- Structured Investment Vehicles (SIVs)
- Credit Hedge Funds
- Money Market Mutual Funds
- Security Lenders
- Limited-purpose Finance Companies (LPFCs)
- Government Sponsored Enterprises (GSEs).

The Federal Reserve Bank of New York Staff Reports no. 458 on *Shadow Banking* concludes the following:
- The volume of credit intermediated by the shadow banking system is of greater magnitude than credit intermediated by the traditional banking system.
- The shadow banking system can be subdivided into three sub-systems which intermediate different types of credit, in fundamentally different ways.
- Some segments of the shadow banking system have emerged through various channels of arbitrage with limited economic value.
- Equally large segments of shadow banking have been driven by gains from specialization. It is more appropriate to refer to these segments as the "parallel" banking system.
- The shadow banking system was temporarily brought into the "daylight" of public liquidity and liability insurance (like traditional banks) but was then pushed back into the shadows.
- Shadow banks will always exist. Their omnipresence—through arbitrage, innovation, and gains from specialization—is a standard feature of all advanced financial systems.

- Regulation by function is a more potent style of regulation than regulation by institutional charter. Regulation by function could have "caught" shadow banks earlier.

Financialization of the economy

In the US the financial sector expansion has gone from 4 times the value of the US GDP in 1980, to 8 times by 2021. To understand the impact of this expansion, trading in US financial markets in 2021 represented: 1.6 times GDP in the Stock Markets; 15 times for Bond Markets; and 31 times for Derivative markets.

This is the consequence of a process known as the Financialization of the economy, where finance, financial markets and financial institutions have an increasing importance in the workings of the economy. This means that financial products and services have a growing impact on the finances of governments, corporations, and households.

As the financial sector has grown significantly and many of the guardrails have loosened or disappeared (Deregulation), the economies' financial fragility has grown, as evidenced by the occurrence of a greater number of financial crises.

Financial Crisis

A financial crisis is defined as any situation where one or more significant financial assets lose a substantial amount of their nominal value.

According to several studies of financial crises, although crises differ in both their nature and severity most commonly occur after a rapid credit expansion, followed by a short period of credit tightening. Once it occurs, a financial crisis usually is impacted by a severe period of economic recession.

It takes some time to recover its economic strength because of the destruction of wealth and income it causes and because as the value of financial assets plummets, the value of liabilities does not change. Historically, it has taken an average of eight years to recover from debt crises.

The most recent financial crises in the US:
- 1980- S & L Crisis.
- 1987- Black Monday stock market crash.
- 2000- Dot-Com stock bubble crash
- 2007- Subprime Mortgage Bubble burst.

Worsening Indebtedness:

The world has been in a process of getting more in debt because governments are borrowing more to cover their fiscal deficits. Also, corporations either have the need to borrow and/or because there are abundant financial resources available, and it is easy to obtain them.

Additionally, households are borrowing either for the purchase of their homes and autos, to pay for their higher education or just to spend through their credit cards.
Whether it is government debt, corporate debt or household debt, the limits and risks apply to all.

Since the debt growth is occurring globally, the impact of the increasing interest rate shock will not only affect borrowers, but also the investors like pension funds, insurance companies, banks, etc. that funded or purchased the securitized loans, so the repercussions will be of a systemic financial crisis.

Potential price shocks.

When the Fed increases interest rates, if the increase is substantial, it will affect not only the economy by causing a drop in business or a recession, but also the financial institutions that loaned them money will face difficulty in getting paid back. If the economy's growth slows down, many borrowers will not be able to repay their debts.

Investors holding long-term bonds are subject to a greater degree of interest rate risk than those holding shorter term bonds. This means that if interest rates change by 1%, long term bonds will see a greater change to their price—rising when rates fall and falling when rates rise.

Rising rates make a bond's future coupon payments worth less, decreasing its current market price. How much more or less is determined by the time the bond reaches maturity.

A greater risk occurs when an increasing amount of mid-term debt is financed with short-term funding and then securitized as is currently occurring. When interest rates rise not only the cost of renewals rise, but also the availability of funds can tighten.

Other debts have adjustable rates, in other words, interest rate increase, so do the adjustable rates. This happened in 2007 with the subprime mortgages.

On the other side of the coin, securitized loans become assets that retirement funds, Insurance Companies and other financial institutions purchase, including Banks.
 So, when repayment of loans or refinancing of loans become difficult, so do the investors' possibilities of recovering their money. By magnifying the volumes of funds securitized into trillions of dollars, the risks are high.

How secure is the global financial system, more than a decade after the 2007-2009 crisis?

Great strides have been made since 2008 to prevent a recurrence of the financial crisis and recession that followed.

Yet there is more debt than ever in the global financial system.

Central banks, regulators, and policy makers were forced to take extraordinary measures after the 2008 crisis. As a result, banks are more highly capitalized today, and less money is moving around the global financial system. But some familiar risks are creeping back, and new ones have emerged.

GLOSSARY

Arbitrage
The simultaneous buying and selling of securities, currency, or commodities in different markets or in derivative forms to take advantage of differing prices for the same asset.

Asset Backed Commercial Paper - ABCP
An asset-backed commercial paper (ABCP) is a short-term investment vehicle with a maturity date that is typically between 90 and 270 days. A bank or other financial institution typically issues the security itself. The notes are backed by the company's physical assets such as trade receivables. Companies will use an asset-backed commercial paper to fund short-term financing needs.

Asset Backed Securities - ABS
ABS are financial securities backed by income-generating assets such as credit card receivables, home equity loans, student loans, and auto loans. ABSs are created when a company sells its loans or other debts to an issuer, a financial institution that then packages them into a portfolio to sell to investors.

Balance of Trade
The balance of trade (BOT), also known as the trade balance, refers to the difference between the monetary value of a country's imports and exports over a given time period. A positive trade balance indicates a trade surplus, while a negative trade balance indicates a trade deficit.

Bonds
A bond is a debt security, similar to an IOU. Borrowers issue bonds to raise money from investors willing to lend them money for a certain amount of time.

Bubble
When the price of an asset rises far higher than can be explained by fundamentals, such as the income likely to derive from holding the asset. Famous bubbles include tulip

mania in Holland during the 17th century, when the prices of tulip bulbs reached unheard of levels, and the South Sea Bubble in Britain a century later, although there have been many others since, including the dotcom bubble in internet company shares that burst in 2000.

Business Cycle

Boom and bust. The long-run pattern of economic growth and recession. According to the Centre for International Business Cycle Research at Columbia University, between 1854 and 1945 the average expansion lasted 29 months and the average contraction 21 months. Since the second world war, however, expansions have lasted almost twice as long, an average of 50 months, and contractions have shortened to an average of only 11 months. A Kitchin cycle supposedly lasted 39 months and was due to fluctuations in companies' inventories. The Juglar cycle would last 8-9 years as a result of changes in investment in plant and machinery. Then there was the 20-year Kuznets cycle, allegedly driven by housebuilding and perhaps the best-known theory of them all, the 50-year Kondratieff wave.

Capital

Economists describe capital as one of the four essential ingredients of economic activity, the factors of production, along with land, labor and enterprise. Production processes that use a lot of capital relative to labor are capital intensive; those that use comparatively little capital are labor intensive.

Capital takes different forms. A firm's assets are known as its capital, which may include fixed capital (machinery, buildings and so on) and working capital (stocks of raw materials and part-finished products, as well as money, which are used up quickly in the production process). Financial capital includes money, bonds and shares. Human capital is the economic wealth or potential contained in a person, some of it endowed at birth, the rest the product of training and education.

Capital Gains
Is an economic concept defined as the profit earned from the sale of an asset which has increased in value over the holding period. An asset may include tangible property, a car, a business, or intangible property such as shares.

Capital Structure
The composition of a company's mixture of debt and equity financing.

Central Bank
A central bank sets short-term interest rates and oversees the health of the financial system, including by acting as lender of last resort to commercial banks that get into financial difficulties.

Collateralized Debt Obligations - CDO
Financial tools that banks use to repackage individual loans into products sold to investors on the secondary market. The value of CDOs comes from the promise of future repayments of the underlying loans.

Commodity
It usually refers to a raw material - oil, cotton, cocoa, silver Commodities are often traded on commodity exchanges.

Complementary Goods
Two products, for which an increase (or fall) in demand for one lead to an increase (fall) in demand for the other. For instance, when you buy a computer, you will also need to buy software. Computer hardware and software are therefore complementary goods.

Concentration
Refers to industries where most of their markets are dominated by a few big firms.

Consumer Prices
The prices paid by whoever finally consumes goods or services.

Crowding Out
Excessive government borrowing causes either borrowing costs to increase or scarcity of funds, displacing private sector borrowing.

Congressional Budget Office - CBO
The Congressional Budget Office (CBO) is a federal agency within the legislative branch of the United States government that provides budget and economic information to Congress.

Consumer Credit
A line of credit extended for personal, or household use Credit extended to an individual for the purchase of consumer goods and services.

Consumption
Consumption expenditure in the private sector accounts for two-thirds of the Gross Domestic Product (GDP). Private consumption is divided into three categories: Durable goods that are defined as goods with a lifetime greater than three years, services that include travel and car repairs, and non-durable goods such as food and water that can be immediately consumed.

Deficit
When more money goes out than comes in. A budget deficit occurs when public spending exceeds government revenue.

Defined Benefit (DB) Retirement Plans
A defined-benefit plan is an employer-sponsored retirement plan where employee benefits are computed using a formula that considers several factors, such as length of employment and salary history.

Defined Contribution Retirement Plans
A Defined Contribution (DC) plan is a retirement plan that's typically tax-deferred, like a 401(k) or a 403(b), in which employees contribute a fixed amount or a percentage of their paychecks to an account that is intended to fund their retirements. The sponsor company will, at times, match a portion of employee contributions as an added benefit.

Deflation
Deflation is a persistent fall in the general price level of goods and services. It is not to be confused with a decline in prices in one economic sector or with a fall in the inflation rate (which is known as disinflation).

Deindustrialization
It's a process in which the industrial activity in a country or region is transferred to another country or reduced because of a major economic or social change.

Demand
Demand is not just about measuring what people want; for economists, it refers to the amount of a good or service that people are both willing and able to buy.

Depression
A prolonged recession in economic activity. The most famous example is the Great Depression of the 1930s. The American economy (among others) went into prolonged recession. Output fell by 30%. unemployment soared and stayed high: in 1939 the jobless rate was still 17% of the workforce. Roughly half of the 25,000 banks in the United States failed.

Deregulation
The process of removing legal or quasi-legal restrictions on the sorts of business done within a particular industry. During the last two decades of the 20th century, many governments committed to the free market pursued policies of liberalization

based on deregulation. The aim was to decrease the role of government in the economy and to increase competition.

Depository Institutions
A financial institution that obtains its funds mainly through deposits from the public. This includes commercial banks, savings and loan associations and credit unions.

Derivatives
Financial instruments that 'derive' their value from another underlying asset. Essentially that means the derivative has no value on its own, other than being an agreement. Instead, the value is perceived from the corresponding asset that it is tied to something that is based on another source.

Dow Jones Industrial Index - DJIA
Is a stock market index of 30 prominent companies listed on stock exchanges in the United States. The DJIA is one of the oldest and most commonly followed equity indices

Economic Deceleration
Means slowing down of economic growth rate.

Economics Definition of Investment
Investment is the spending by firms on new factories, office buildings, machinery and inventories, plus spending by households on new houses.

Employee Retirement Income Security Act - ERISA
A federal law that protects the retirement assets of American workers. The law, which was enacted in 1974, implemented rules that qualified plans must follow to ensure that plan fiduciaries do not misuse plan assets.

Equities
Equities are shares of a company's ownership when referring to the stock market. As a result, when a corporation offers equity, it is selling a portion of its ownership.

Exchange Rate
The price at which one currency can be converted into another.

Factors of Production
The ingredients of economic activity: land, labor, capital and enterprise.

Fannie Mae
The Federal National Mortgage Association (FNMA), commonly known as Fannie Mae, is a United States government-sponsored enterprise (GSE) the corporation's purpose is to expand the secondary mortgage market by securitizing mortgage loans in the form of mortgage-backed securities (MBS),[4] allowing lenders to reinvest their assets into more lending and in effect increasing the number of lenders in the mortgage market by reducing the reliance on locally based savings and loan associations (or "thrifts").

Federal Housing Administration - FHA
A part of the U.S. Department of Housing and Urban Development. It provides mortgage insurance on loans made by FHA-approved lenders. It insures mortgages on single family homes, multifamily properties, residential care facilities, and hospitals throughout the United States and its territories.

Federal Reserve - FED
The Federal Reserve System is the central bank of the United States. It conducts the nation's monetary policy to promote maximum employment, stable prices, and moderate long-term interest rates in the U.S. economy.

Financial Intermediation
A financial institution such as a commercial bank or thrift that facilitates the flow of funds from savers to borrowers. A financial intermediary is an entity that acts as the middleman between two parties in a financial transaction, such as a

commercial bank, investment bank, mutual fund, or pension fund.

Financialization
Refers to the increase in size and importance of a country's financial sector relative to its overall economy. The term also describes not just the increase of the market and financial sector's presence in our lives but the increasing diversity of transactions and market players as well as their intersection with all parts of the economy and society.

Fiscal Policy
It comprises public spending and taxation, and any other government income or assistance to the private sector (such as tax breaks).

Foreign Direct Investment - FDI
An ownership stake in a foreign company or project made by an investor, company, or government from another country. Generally, the term is used to describe a business decision to acquire a substantial stake in a foreign business or to buy it outright to expand operations to a new region.

Freddie Mac
The Federal Home Loan Mortgage Corp. (FHLMC) is a stockholder-owned, government-sponsored enterprise (GSE) chartered by Congress in 1970 to keep money flowing to mortgage lenders. The FHLMC, familiarly known as Freddie Mac, its role is to buy loans from mortgage lenders, then combine them and sell them as mortgage-backed securities.

Full Employment
Full employment refers to everyone who wants work and is willing to work. This does not mean zero unemployment, because at any point in time some people do not want to work. Also, because some people are always between jobs, there will usually be some frictional unemployment.

Gini Coefficient
The Gini coefficient measures the inequality of income distribution within a country. It varies from zero, which indicates perfect equality, with every household earning the same, to one which implies absolute inequality, with a single household earning a country's entire income.

Global Debt
Global debt refers to the total debt by governments, businesses and people.

Globalization
Refers to the trend for people, firms and governments around the world to become increasingly dependent on and integrated with each other, brought about by cross-border trade in goods and services, technology, and flows of investment, people, and information.

Government Sponsored Enterprises - GSE
A quasi-governmental entity established to enhance the flow of credit to specific sectors of the American economy. Government-sponsored enterprises (GSEs) do not lend money to the public directly; instead, they guarantee third-party loans and purchase loans in the secondary market, ensuring liquidity.

Gross Domestic Product - GDP
The total monetary or market value of all the finished goods and services produced within a country's borders in a specific time period.

Gross National Product - GNP
Short for gross national product, another measure of a country's economic performance. It is calculated by adding to GDP the income earned by residents from investments abroad, less the corresponding income sent home by foreigners who are living in the country.

Hedge
Reducing your risks. Hedging involves deliberately taking on a new risk that offsets an existing one, such as your exposure to an adverse change in an exchange rate, interest rate or commodity price.

Hedge Funds
A hedge fund is a limited partnership of private investors whose money is managed by professional fund managers who use a wide range of strategies, including leveraging or trading of non-traditional assets, to earn above-average investment returns.

Hyper-inflation
Rapid, excessive, and out-of-control general price increases in an economy.

Income Inequality
Income inequality refers to how unevenly income is distributed throughout a population. The less equal the distribution, the higher income inequality is. Income inequality is often accompanied by wealth inequality, which is the uneven distribution of wealth.

Indexation
Keeping pace with inflation. in many countries, wages, pensions, unemployment benefits and some other sorts of income are automatically raised according to recent movements in the consumer price index.

Individual Retirement Accounts - IRA's
Retirement savings accounts with tax advantages. Types of IRAs include traditional IRAs, Roth IRAs, Simplified Employee Pension (SEP) IRAs, and Savings Incentive Match Plan for Employees (SIMPLE) IRAs.

Investment
An investment is an asset or item acquired with the goal of generating income or appreciation. Appreciation refers to an increase in the value of an asset over time. When an individual purchases a good as an investment, the intent is not to consume the good but rather to use it in the future to create wealth.

Investment Grade
Investment grade refers to the quality of a company's credit. To be considered an investment grade issue, the company must be rated at 'BBB' or higher by Standard and Poor's or Moody's. Credit ratings provide a useful measure for comparing fixed-income securities, such as bonds, bills, and notes. Most companies receive ratings according to their financial strengths, prospects, and past history. Companies that have manageable levels of debt, good earnings potential, and good debt-paying records will have good credit ratings. Anything below this 'BBB' rating is considered non-investment grade. If the company or bond is rated 'BB' or lower it is known as junk grade, in which case the probability that the company will repay its issued debt is deemed to be speculative.

Junk Bonds
Junk bonds, also known as high-yield bonds, are bonds that are rated below investment grade by the big three rating agencies. Junk bonds carry a higher risk of default than other bonds, but they pay higher returns to make them attractive to investors.

Labor
One of the factors of production, with land, capital and enterprise.

Labor Productivity
The productivity of workers measured as a coefficient of

hours of work per product or GDP. It may be further broken down by sector to examine trends in labor growth, wage levels, and technological improvement.

Corporate profits and shareholder returns are directly linked to productivity growth. At the corporate level, productivity is a measure of the efficiency of a company's production process, it is calculated by measuring the number of units produced relative to employee labor hours or by measuring a company's net sales relative to employee labor hours.

Macro Prudential Measures

Macroprudential measures aim to increase the
financial system's resilience to shocks by addressing possible systemic risks. Macroprudential authorities monitor the financial system, identifying risks and vulnerabilities, and take measures to ensure financial stability.

Macroeconomic Policy

Policy by government and central banks, usually intended to maximize growth while keeping down inflation and unemployment. The main instruments of macroeconomic policy are changes in the rate of interest and money supply, known as monetary policy, and changes in taxation and public spending, known as fiscal policy.

Medicare

Medicare is the federal government health insurance program for people aged 65 and older and younger people living with certain illnesses or disabilities. Medicare consists of four parts — Part A, Part B, Part C and Part D. Each part offers specific coverage and varies in cost:
- Part A covers hospital care and related services.
- Part B covers doctor appointments and outpatient medical care.
- Part C covers the same benefits as Parts A and B but is offered by private insurers.
- Part D covers prescription drugs

Microeconomics
Studies the behavior and decision-making of individuals and firms in response to changes in incentives, prices, resources, and methods of production.

Money Market Account
A money market account (MMA) is a savings account. Money market accounts tend to offer a higher interest rate than traditional savings accounts. Typically, money market accounts also have higher minimum balance requirements.

Money Market Funds - MMF
A money market fund is a kind of mutual fund that invests in highly liquid, near-term instruments. These instruments include cash, cash equivalent securities, and high-credit-rating, debt-based securities with a short-term maturity (such as U.S. Treasuries). Money market funds are intended to offer investors high liquidity with a very low level of risk. Money market funds are also called money market mutual funds. A money market fund is an investment that is sponsored by an investment fund company. Therefore, it carries no guarantee of principal.

Monetary Policy
Monetary policy involves open-market operations, reserve requirements and changing the short-term rate of interest (the discount rate).

Mortgage
A mortgage is a debt instrument, secured by the collateral of specified real estate property, that the borrower is obliged to pay back with a predetermined set of payments.

Mortgage-Backed Securities - MBS
Mortgage-backed securities, called MBS, are bonds secured by home and other real estate loans. They are created when a number of these loans, usually with similar characteristics, are pooled together.

Mutual Funds

A mutual fund is a company that pools money from many investors and invests the money in securities such as stocks, bonds, and short-term debt. The combined holdings of the mutual fund are known as its portfolio. Investors buy shares in mutual funds. Each share represents an investor's part ownership in the fund and the income it generates. The price of the mutual fund, also known as its net asset value (NAV) is determined by the total value of the securities in the portfolio, divided by the number of the fund's outstanding shares. This price fluctuates based on the value of the securities held by the portfolio at the end of each business day. Note that mutual fund investors do not actually own the securities in which the fund invests; they only own shares in the fund itself.

Net Investment

In economics, net investment is spending which increases the availability of fixed capital goods or means of production and goods inventories. It is the total spending on newly produced physical capital (fixed investment) and on inventories (inventory investment)—that is, gross investment—minus replacement investment, which simply replaces depreciated capital goods. It is productive capital formation plus net additions to the stock of housing and the stock of inventories.

Non-Depository Intermediaries

Are financial institutions that don't take deposits. Instead, they perform other financial services and collect fees for them as their primary means of business.

Organization of Oil Exporting Countries - OPEC

OPEC is a multinational organization that was established to coordinate the petroleum policies of its members. Its founding countries include Algeria, Angola, Equatorial Guinea, Gabon, Iran, Iraq, Kuwait, Libya, Nigeria, the Republic of the Congo, Saudi Arabia, the United Arab Emirates and Venezuela. Ecuador, Indonesia, and Qatar are former OPEC members.

A larger group called OPEC+ was formed in late 2016 to have more control on the global crude oil market.

Output Gap
Refers to how far an economy's current output is below what it would be at full capacity.

Over-the Counter - OTC
Refers to buying and selling securities outside of an official stock exchange. OTC investments can include penny stocks, bonds, derivatives, ADRs, and currencies. OTC markets are electronic networks that allow two parties to trade with each other using a dealer-broker as an intermediary.

Pensions
A pension is a retirement plan that provides a monthly income. A pension is a steady income given to a person (usually after retirement). Pensions are typically payments made in the form of a guaranteed annuity to a retired or disabled employee. The employer bears all of the risk and responsibility for funding the plan.

Potential GDP
The Potential GDP definition states that it is the level of GDP that is possible or attainable while the economy is operating at a maximum resource usage rate over a period of time. It represents full employment GDP and gauges the economy's productive capability, especially at a constant inflation ratio.

Productivity
Productivity, in economics, measures output per unit of input, such as labor, capital, or any other resource. It is often calculated for the economy as a ratio of gross domestic product (GDP) to hours worked.

Public Debt
The U.S. Public (national) Debt is the sum total of all outstanding Treasury Bonds and Notes sold at auction by

U.S. Department of Treasury to both finance the annual U.S. Federal Budget Deficit (the shortfall of federal tax revenues as compared to federal government expenditures) and pay Debt Service (interest) on the public (national) debt.

Public Goods
Things that can be consumed by everybody in a society. Examples include clean air, a national defense system and the judiciary.

Public Sector Deficit
Public Sector Deficit refers to a situation in which government spending exceeds taxes collected. That is, a public sector deficit occurs when a government spends more than it receives in a given period of time, usually a year.

Public Utility
A firm providing essential services to the public, such as water, electricity and postal services, usually involving elements of natural monopoly.

Recession
A period of slow or negative economic growth, usually accompanied by rising unemployment for two consecutive quarters of falling GDP.

Securities
Securities are fungible and tradable financial instruments used to raise capital in public and private markets. There are primarily three types of securities: equity—which provides ownership rights to holders; debt—essentially loans repaid with periodic payments; and hybrids—which combine aspects of debt and equity.

A security can represent ownership in a corporation in the form of stock, a creditor relationship with a governmental body or a corporation represented by owning that entity's bond; or rights to ownership as represented by an option.

Service Sector

The tertiary sector, also known as the service sector, involves a variety of things. it comprises various service industries including warehousing and transportation services; information services; securities and other investment services; professional services; waste management; health care and social assistance; and arts, entertainment, and recreation.

Shadow Banking

The shadow banking system is a term for the collection of non-bank financial intermediaries (NBFIs) that provide services similar to traditional commercial banks but outside normal banking regulations. The shadow banking system is a group of financial intermediaries which facilitate the creation of credit across the global financial system, but whose members are not subject to regulatory oversight. These companies are often known as nonbank financial companies (NBFCs). The shadow banking system also refers to unregulated activities by regulated institutions.

Standard and Poor - S & P 500

The Standard and Poor's 500 is a free-float weighted measurement stock market index of 500 of the largest companies listed on stock exchanges in the United States. The S&P 500 Index measures the value of the stocks of the 500 largest corporations by market capitalization listed on the New York Stock Exchange or Nasdaq. The S&P 500 is meant to provide a barometer of the U.S. stock market and economy, covering approximately 80% of available market capitalization.

Stock Buybacks

A stock buyback is when a public company uses cash to buy shares of its own stock on the open market. A stock buyback (also known as a share repurchase) is a process when a company buys back its shares from the marketplace, therefore reducing the number of shares that are outstanding.

Structured Investment Vehicles - SIV

A structured investment vehicle (SIV) is a pool of investment assets that attempts to profit from credit spreads between short-term debt and long-term structured finance products such as asset-backed securities (ABS).A SIV, administered by a commercial bank or another asset manager such as a hedge fund, will issue asset-backed commercial paper (ABCP) to fund the purchase of these securities.

Unemployment

The number of people of working age without a job is usually expressed as an unemployment rate, as a percentage of the workforce. There are also voluntary unemployment and involuntary unemployment.

Value Added

This usually refers to firms, where it is defined as the value of the firm's output minus the value of all its inputs purchased from other firms.

Windfall Profit

A profit that in theory is earned unexpectedly, through circumstances beyond the control of the company concerned.

REFERENCES

References on Economic Growth

1. Basic References

Barro, Robert J. and Xavier Sala-i-Martin, Economic Growth, McGraw-Hill, 1995.

Jones, Charles I., Introduction to Economic Growth, New York: W.W. Norton and Co.,2002. Second Edition.

Romer, David, Advanced Macroeconomics, New York: McGraw-Hill, 1996.

Aghion, Philippe and Peter Howitt, Endogenous Growth Theory, Cambridge, MA: MIT Press, 1998.

Grossman, Gene M. and Elhanan Helpman, Innovation and Growth in the Global Economy, Cambridge, MA: MIT Press, 1991.

Articles by Romer, Grossman-Helpman, Solow, and Pack, "Symposium on New Growth Theory," Journal of Economic Perspectives, Winter 1994.

2. Internet Resources

Jones, Charles I., "Chad's Growth Resources," (This list, plus many more links). http://elsa.berkeley.edu/~chad/growth.html.

Temple, Jonathan, "Economic Growth Resources," University of Bristol. http://www.bris.ac.uk/Depts/Economics/Growth/. This is the most thorough collection of growth resources available, including a good list of references and surveys.

3. Neoclassical Growth Models

Basic References

Solow, Robert M., "A Contribution to the Theory of Economic Growth," Quarterly Journal of Economics, February 1956, 70, 65–94.

Ramsey, Frank, "A Mathematical Theory of Saving," Economic Journal, 1928, 38, 543–559.

Cass, David, "Optimal Growth in an Aggregative Model of Capital Accumulation, "Review of Economic Studies, July 1965, 32, 233–240.

Koopmans, T. C., "On the Concept of Optimal Economic Growth," in "The Econometric Approach to Development Planning," Amsterdam: North Holland, 1965.

King, Robert and Sergio Rebelo, "Transitional Dynamics and Economic Growth in the Neoclassical Model," American Economic Review, 1993, 83, 908–931.

Diamond, Peter, "National Debt in a Neoclassical Growth Model," American Economic Review, 1965, 55, 1126–1150.

Blanchard, Olivier J., "Debts, Deficits, and Finite Horizons," Journal of Political Economy, 1985, 93 (2), 223–247.

Optimal Control and Dynamic Optimization

Barro, Robert J. and Xavier Sala-i-Martin, Economic Growth, McGraw-Hill, 1995. (Especially Appendix 1.3).

Kamien, Morton I. and Nancy L. Schwartz, Dynamic Optimization: The Calculus of Variations and Optimal Control in Economics and Management, North Holland,1991.

Arrow, Kenneth and Mordecai Kurz, Public Investment, the Rate of Return, and Optimal Fiscal Policy, Baltimore: Johns Hopkins University Press, 1970.

Romer, Paul M., "Cake Eating, Chattering, and Jumps: Existence Results for Variational Problems," Econometrica, 1986, 54, 897–908.

Kamihigashi, Takashi, "Necessity of Transversality Conditions for Infinite Horizon Problems," Econometrica, Forthcoming 2001.

4. Empirical Evidence: Growth and Levels

Data

Summers, Robert, and Alan Heston, "The Penn World Table (Mark 5): An Expanded Set of International Comparisons: 1950–1988," Quarterly Journal of Economics, May 1991, 106, 327–368.

Maddison, Angus, Monitoring the World Economy 1820-1992, Paris: Organization for Economic Cooperation and Development, 1995.

Surveys

McGrattan, Ellen and James Schmitz, "Explaining Cross-Country Income Differences." In Taylor Woodford. Dauerlauf, Steven, and Danny Quah, "The New Empirics of Economic Growth." In Taylor Woodford.

Temple, Jonathan, "The new growth evidence," Journal of Economic Literature, March 1999, 37 (1), 112–156.

Taylor, John B. and Michael Woodford, eds, North-Holland Elsevier Science, 1999.

Growth Accounting

Solow, Robert M., "Technical Change and the Aggregate Production Function," Review of Economics and Statistics, August 1957, 39 (3), 312–320.

Denison, Edward F., The Sources of Economic Growth in the United States and the Alternatives Before Us, New York: Committee for Economic Development, 1962.

W., Frank M. Gollop Jorgenson Dale, and Barbara M. Fraumeni, Productivity and U.S. Economic Growth, Cambridge, MA: Harvard University Press, 1987.

Hall, Robert E., "Invariance Properties of Solow's Productivity Residual," in Peter Diamond, ed., Growth/Productivity/Unemployment: Essays to Celebrate Robert Solow's Birthday, Cambridge, MA: MIT Press, 1990, pp. 71–112.

Young, Alwyn, "A Tale of Two Cities: Factor Accumulation and Technical Change in Hong Kong and Singapore," in Olivier Blanchard and Stanley Fischer, eds., NBER Macroeconomics Annual, Cambridge, MA: MIT Press, 1992, pp. 13–54., "The Tyranny of Numbers: Confronting the Statistical Realities of the East Asian Growth Experience," Quarterly Journal of Economics, August 1995, 110 (3), 641–680.

Klenow, Peter, and Andres Rodriguez-Clare, "The Neoclassical Revival in Growth Economics: Has It Gone Too Far?" in Ben S. Bernanke and Julio J. Rotenberg, eds., NBER Macroeconomics Annual 1997, Cambridge, MA: MIT Press, 1997.

Abramovitz, Moses and Paul A. David, "American Macroeconomic Growth in the Era of Knowledge-Based Progress," 1998. Stanford University mimeo.

Bosworth, Barry P., and Susan M. Collins, "Capital Flows to Developing Countries: Implications for Saving and Investment," Brookings Papers on Economic Activity,1999, 1, 143–180.

Growth Regressions and Convergence

Baumol, William J., "Productivity Growth, Convergence and Welfare: What the Long-Run Data Show," American Economic Review, December 1986, 76, 1072–1085.

DeLong, J. Bradford, "Productivity Growth, Convergence, and Welfare: Comment, "American Economic Review, 1988, 78, 1138–1154.

Barro, Robert J., "Economic Growth in a Cross Section of Countries," Quarterly Journal of Economics, May 1991, 106, 407–443.

Mankiw, N. Gregory, David Romer, and David Weil, "A Contribution to the Empirics of Economic Growth," Quarterly Journal of Economics, May 1992, 107 (2), 407– 438.

Barro, Robert J. and Xavier Sala-i-Martin, "Convergence," Journal of Political Economy, 1992, 100 (2), 223–251., and "Convergence Across States and Regions," Brookings Papers on Economic Activity, 1991, pp. 107–158.

Levine, Ross, and David Renelt, "A Sensitivity Analysis of Cross-Country Growth Regressions," American Economic Review, September 1992, 82 (4), 942–963.

Sala-i-Martin, Xavier, "I Just Ran Two Million Regressions," American Economic Association Papers and Proceedings, May 1997, 87 (2), 178–183.

Bernard, Andrew B. and Charles I. Jones, "Comparing Apples to Oranges: Productivity Convergence and Measurement across Industries and Countries," American Economic Review, December 1996, 86 (5), 1216–1238.

Easterly, William, Michael Kremer, Lant Pritchett, and Lawrence Summers, "Good Policy or Good Luck? Country Growth Performance and Temporary Shocks," Journal of Monetary Economics, December 1993, 32, 459–483.

Mankiw, N. Gregory, "The Growth of Nations," Brookings Papers on Economic Activity, 1995, 1, 275–326.

Islam, Nazrul, "Growth Empirics: A Panel Data Approach," Quarterly Journal of Economics, November 1995, 110, 1127–1170.

Caselli, Francesco, Gerardo Esquivel, and Fernando Lefort, "Reopening the Convergence Debate: A New Look at Cross-Country Growth Empirics," Journal of Economic Growth, September 1996, 1, 363–390.

Barro, Robert J., Determinants of Economic Growth: A Cross-country Empirical Study, Cambridge, MA: MIT Press, 1997.

Bils, Mark, and Peter Klenow, "Does Schooling Cause Growth?" American Economic Review, December 2000, 90, 1160–1183.

Levels, Productivity, and Distributions

Lucas, Robert E., "Why Doesn't Capital Flow from Rich to Poor Countries," American Economic Association Papers and Proceedings, May 1990, 80, 92–96.

Mankiw, N. Gregory, David Romer, and David Weil, "A Contribution to the Empirics of Economic Growth," Quarterly Journal of Economics, May 1992, 107 (2), 407–438.

Hall, Robert E. and Charles I. Jones, "Why Do Some Countries Produce So Much More Output per Worker than Others?" Quarterly Journal of Economics, February 1999, 114 (1), 83–116.

Klenow, Peter and Andres Rodriguez-Clare, "The Neoclassical Revival in Growth Economics: Has It Gone Too Far?" in Ben S. Bernanke and Julio J. Rotenberg, eds., NBER Macroeconomics Annual 1997, Cambridge, MA: MIT Press, 1997.

Pritchett, Lant, "Divergence: Big Time," Journal of Economic Perspectives, Summer 1997, 11 (3), 3–17.

Prescott, Edward C., "Needed: A Theory of Total Factor Productivity," 1997. Federal Reserve Bank of Minneapolis, Staff Report 242.

Jones, Charles I., "On the Evolution of the World Income Distribution," Journal of Economic Perspectives, Summer 1997, 11, 19–36.

Clark, Gregory, "Why Isn't the Whole World Developed? Lessons from the Cotton Mills," Journal of Economic History, March 1987, 47, 141–173. and Robert Feenstra, "Technology in the Great Divergence," in "Globalization in Historical Perspective," University of Chicago Press, forthcoming. Http://www.nber.org/ confer/2001/globes01/clark.pdf.

Quah, Danny, "Galton's Fallacy and Tests of the Convergence Hypothesis," Scandinavian Journal of Economics, December 1993, 95, 427–443., "Twin Peaks: Growth and Convergence in Models of Distribution Dynamics, "Economic Journal, July 1996, 106 (437), 1045–1055.

Parente, Stephen L. and Edward C. Prescott, "Changes in the Wealth of Nations," Federal Reserve Bank of Minneapolis Quarterly Review, Spring 1993, pp. 3–16. and "Monopoly

Rights: A Barrier to Riches," American Economic Review, December 1999, 89 (5), 1216–1233.

Chari, V.V., Pat Kehoe, and Ellen McGrattan, "The Poverty of Nations: A Quantitative Investigation," 1997. Working Paper, Federal Reserve Bank of Minneapolis.

Ciccone, Antonio, and Robert E. Hall, "Productivity and the Density of Economic Activity," American Economic Review, March 1996, 86 (1), 54–70.

Frankel, Jeffrey A. and David Romer, "Does Trade Cause Growth?" American Economic Review, June 1999, 89 (3), 379–399.

Restuccia, Deigo and Carlos Urrutia, "Relative Prices and Investment Rates," Journal of Monetary Economics, February 2001, 47 (1), 93–121.

Acemoglu, Daron and Fabrizio Zilibotti, "Productivity Differences," Quarterly Journal of Economics, 2001, 116 (2), 563–606.

Caselli, Francesco, and Wilbur John Coleman, "The World Technology Frontier," September 2000. NBER Working Paper No. 7904.

Acemoglu, Daron, Simon Johnson, and James A. Robinson, "The Colonial Origins of Comparative Development: An Empirical Investigation," American Economic Review, December 2001, 91 (5), 1369–1401, and "Reversal of Fortune: Geography and Institutions in the Making of the Modern World Income Distribution," 2001. MIT Working Paper.

5. First Generation/ "AK" Growth Models

Frankel, Marvin, "The Production Function in Allocation and Growth: A Synthesis, American Economic Review, December 1962, 52, 995–1022.

Sheshinski, Eytan, "Optimal Accumulation with Learning by Doing," in Karl Shell, ed., Essays on the Theory of Economic Growth, Cambridge, MA: MIT Press, 1967.

Romer, Paul M., "Crazy Explanations for the Productivity Slowdown," in Stanley Fischer, ed., NBER Macroeconomics Annual 1987, Cambridge, MA: MIT Press,1987.

Lucas, Robert E., "On the Mechanics of Economic Development," Journal of Monetary Economics, 1988, 22 (1), 3–42.

Romer, Paul M., "Capital Accumulation in the Theory of Long Run Growth," in Robert J. Barro, ed., Modern Business Cycle Theory, Cambridge, MA: Harvard University Press, 1989.

Rebelo, Sergio, "Long-Run Policy Analysis and Long-Run Growth," Journal of Political Economy, June 1991, 99, 500–521.

Barro, Robert J., "Government Spending in a Simple Model of Endogenous Growth," Journal of Political Economy, October 1990, 98, S103–S125.

6. Idea-Based Growth Models

<u>Basic References.</u>

Romer, Paul M., "Endogenous Technological Change," Journal of Political Economy, October 1990, 98 (5), S71–S102., "Increasing Returns and Long-Run Growth," Journal of Political Economy, October 1986, 94, 1002–1037.

Phelps, Edmund S., "Models of Technical Progress and the Golden Rule of Research," Review of Economic Studies, April 1966, 33, 133–45.

Shell, Karl, "Toward a Theory of Inventive Activity and Capital Accumulation," American Economic Association Papers and Proceedings, 1966, 56, 62–68.

Nordhaus, William D., "An Economic Theory of Technological Change," American Economic Association Papers and Proceedings, May 1969, 59, 18–28.

Judd, Kenneth L., "On the Performance of Patents," Econometrica, May 1985, 53 (3), 567–585.

Romer, Paul M., "Growth Based on Increasing Returns to Specialization," American Economic Review Papers and Proceedings, May 1987, 77, 56–62.

Aghion, Philippe and Peter Howitt, "A Model of Growth through Creative Destruction," Econometrica, March 1992, 60 (2), 323–351.

Grossman, Gene M. and Elhanan Helpman, Innovation and Growth in the Global Economy, Cambridge, MA: MIT Press, 1991.

Jones, Charles I., "R&D-Based Models of Economic Growth," Journal of Political Economy, August 1995, 103 (4), 759–784.

Kortum, Samuel S., "Research, Patenting, and Technological Change," Econometrica, 1997, 65 (6), 1389–1419.

Weitzman, Martin L., "Recombinant Growth," Quarterly Journal of Economics, May 1998, 113, 331–360.

Scale Effects and Idea-Based Growth

Jones, Charles I., "R&D-Based Models of Economic Growth," Journal of Political Economy, August 1995, 103 (4), 759–784., "Population and Ideas: A Theory of Endogenous Growth," December 1998. Stanford University mimeo.

Kremer, Michael, "Population Growth and Technological Change: One Million B.C. to 1990," Quarterly Journal of Economics, August 1993, 108 (4), 681–716.

Young, Alwyn, "Growth without Scale Effects," Journal of Political Economy, February 1998, 106 (1), 41–63.

Dinopoulos, Elias and Peter Thompson, "Schumpeterian Growth without Scale Effects," Journal of Economic Growth, December 1998, 3 (4), 313–335.

Segerstrom, Paul, "Endogenous Growth Without Scale Effects," American Economic Review, December 1998, 88 (5), 1290–1310.

Peretto, Pietro, "Technological Change and Population Growth," Journal of Economic Growth, December 1998, 3 (4), 283–311.

Howitt, Peter, "Steady Endogenous Growth with Population and R&D Inputs Growing," Journal of Political Economy, August 1999, 107 (4), 715–730.

Jones, Charles I., "Growth: With or Without Scale Effects?" American Economic Association Papers and Proceedings, May 1999, 89, 139–144.

Li, Chol-Won, "Endogenous vs. Semi-Endogenous Growth in a Two-R&D-Sector Model," Economic Journal, March 2000, 110 (462), C109–C122.

7. Empirical Evidence on Models of Long-Run Growth

Jones, Charles I., "Time Series Tests of Endogenous Growth Models," Quarterly Journal of Economics, May 1995, 110 (441), 495–525.

Stokey, Nancy L. and Sergio Rebelo, "Growth Effects of Flat-Rate Taxes," Journal of Political Economy, June 1995, 103, 519–550.

Jones, Charles I., "Sources of U.S. Economic Growth in a World of Ideas," American Economic Review, Forthcoming 2002.

Bils, Mark and Peter Klenow, "Quantifying Quality Growth," American Economic Review, September 2001, 91 (4), 1006–1030.

Costa, Dora L., "Estimating Real Income in the US from 1888 to 1994: Correcting CPI Bias Using Engel Curves," Journal of Political Economy, December 109 (6), 1288–1310.

8. Learning by Doing and Human Capital

Learning by Doing

Arrow, Kenneth J., "The Economic Implications of Learning by Doing," Review of Economic Studies, June 1962, 29, 153–173.

Frankel, Marvin, "The Production Function in Allocation and Growth: A Synthesis," American Economic Review, December 1962, 52, 995–1022.

Sheshinski, Eytan, "Optimal Accumulation with Learning by Doing," in Karl Shell, ed., Essays on the Theory of Economic Growth, Cambridge, MA: MIT Press, 1967.

Lucas, Robert E., "On the Mechanics of Economic Development," Journal of Monetary Economics, 1988, 22 (1), 3–42, "Making a Miracle," Econometrica, 1993, 61, 251–272.

Irwin, Douglas A. and Peter J. Klenow, "Learning-by-doing Spillovers in the Semiconductor Industry," Journal of Political Economy, December 1994, 102 (6).

Foster, Andrew and Mark Rosenzweig, "Learning by Doing and Learning from Others: Human Capital and Technical Change in Agriculture," Journal of Political Economy, 1995, 103, 1176–1209.

Jovanovic, Boyan and Yaw Nyarko, "Learning by Doing and the Choice of Technology," Econometrica, November 1996., "Learning and Growth," in David M. Kreps and Kenneth F. Wallis, eds., Advances in Economics and Econometrics: Theory and Applications, New York: Cambridge University Press, 1997.

Thompson, Peter, "How Much Did the Liberty Shipbuilders Learn? New Evidence for an Old Case Study," Journal of Political Economy, February 2001, 109 (1), 103–137.

Thorton, Rebecca A. and Peter Thompson, "Learning from Experience and Learning from Others. An exploration of learning and spillovers in wartime shipbuilding," American Economic Review, December 2001, 91 (5), 1350–1368.

Human Capital

Lucas, Robert E., "On the Mechanics of Economic Development," Journal of Monetary Economics, 1988, 22 (1), 3–42.

Mankiw, N. Gregory, David Romer, and David Weil, "A Contribution to the Empirics of Economic Growth," Quarterly Journal of Economics, May 1992, 107 (2), 407–438.

Bils, Mark and Peter Klenow, "Does Schooling Cause Growth?" American Economic Review, December 2000, 90, 1160–1183.

Klenow, Peter and Andres Rodriguez-Clare, "The Neoclassical Revival in Growth Economics: Has It Gone Too Far?" in Ben S. Bernanke and Julio J. Rotenberg, eds., NBER Macroeconomics Annual 1997, Cambridge, MA: MIT Press, 1997.

Hall, Robert E. and Charles I. Jones, "Why Do Some Countries Produce So Much More Output per Worker than Others?" Quarterly Journal of Economics, February 1999, 114 (1), 83–116.

9. Why are We So Rich and They So Poor?

See References in Section 4.E

Technology/Ideas Transfer and Diffusion

Nelson, Richard R. and Edmund S. Phelps, "Investment in Humans, Technological Diffusion, and Economic Growth," American Economic Association Papers and Proceedings, May 1966, 56, 69–75.

Krugman, Paul, "A Model of Innovation, Technology Transfer, and the World Distribution of Income," Journal of Political Economy, 1979, 87, 253–266.

Brezis, Elise S., Paul R. Krugman, and Daniel Tsiddon, "Leapfrogging in International Competition: A Theory of Cycles in National Technological Leadership," American Economic Review, December 1993, pp. 1211–1219.

Romer, Paul, "Idea Gaps and Object Gaps in Economic Development," Journal of Monetary Economics, 1993, pp. 543–573.

Romer, Paul M., "Two Strategies for Economic Development: Using Ideas and Producing Ideas," Proceedings of the World Bank Annual Conference on Development Economics, 1992, 1993, pp. 63–115.

"New Goods, Old Theory, and the Welfare Costs of Trade Restrictions," Journal of Development Economics, 1994, 43, 5–38.

Parente, Stephen L. and Edward C. Prescott, "Barriers to Technology Adoption and Development," Journal of Political Economy, April 1994, 102 (2), 298–321.

Barro, Robert J. and Xavier Sala-i-Martin, "Technological Diffusion, Convergence, and Growth," Journal of Economic Growth, 1997, pp. 1–26.

Eaton, Jonathan and Samuel S. Kortum, "Trade in Ideas: Patenting and Productivity in the OECD," 1995. NBER Working Paper No. 5049. International Technology Diffusion: Theory and Measurement," International Economic Review, 1999, 40, 537–570.

Easterly, William, Robert King, Ross Levine, and Sergio Rebelo, "Policy, Technology Adoption and Growth," 1994. NBER Working Paper No. 4681.

Corruption and Political Economy

Baumol, William J., "Entrepreneurship: Productive, Unproductive, and Destructive," Journal of Political Economy, 1990, 98 (5), 893–921.

Murphy, Kevin M., Andrei Shleifer, and Robert W. Vishny, "The Allocation of Talent: Implications for Growth," Quarterly Journal of Economics, May 1991, 106 (2), 503–530.

Shleifer, Andrei and Robert W. Vishny, "Corruption," Quarterly Journal of Economics, August 1993, 108 (3), 599–618.

Mauro, Paolo, "Corruption and Growth," Quarterly Journal of Economics, August 1995, 110 (3), 681–713.

Hall, Robert E. and Charles I. Jones, "Why Do Some Countries Produce So Much More Output per Worker than Others?" Quarterly Journal of Economics, February 1999, 114 (1), 83–116.

Olson, Mancur, "Big Bills Left on the Sidewalk: Why Some Nations are Rich, and Others Poor," Journal of Economic Perspectives, Spring 1996, 10 (2), 3–24.

Krusell, Per and Victor Rios-Rull, "Vested Interests in a Positive Theory of Stagnation and Growth," Review of Economic Studies, 1996, 63, 301–331.

10. The Direction of Technical Change

Skilled vs. Unskilled Labor

Katz, Lawrence and Kevin Murphy, "Changes in Relative Wages, 1963–1987: Supply and Demand Factors," Quarterly Journal of Economics, February 1992, 107 (1), 35–78.

Acemoglu, Daron, "Why Do New Technologies Complement Skills? Directed Technical Change and Wage Inequality," Quarterly Journal of Economics, 1998, 113, 1055–1089.

Murphy, Kevin, Craig Riddell, and Paul Romer, "Wages, Skills and Technology in the United States and Canada," in Elhanan Helpman, ed., General Purpose Technologies and Economic Growth, Cambridge: MIT Press, 1998.

Krusell, Per, Lee Ohanian, Jose-Victor Rios-Rull, and Giovanni Violante, "Capital Skill Complementarity and Inequality: A Macroeconomic Analysis," Econometrica, September 2000, 68 (5), 1029–1053.

Galor, Oded and Omer Moav, "Ability Biased Technological Transition, Wage Inequality, and Economic Growth," Quarterly Journal of Economics, May 2000, 115, 469–498.

Acemoglu, Daron and Fabrizio Zilibotti, "Productivity Differences," Quarterly Journal of Economics, 2001, 116 (2), 563–606.

"Directed Technical Change," 2001. NBER Working Paper No. 8287. "Labor- and Capital-Augmenting Technical Change," July 2001. MIT mimeo.

Investment-Specific Technical Change

Greenwood, Jeremy, Zvi Hercowitz, and Per Krusell, "Long-Run Implications of Investment-Specific Technological Change," American Economic Review, June 1997, 87 (3), 342–362.

Whelan, Karl, "Balance Growth Revisited: A Two-Sector Model of Economic Growth," 2001. Federal Reserve Board of Governors mimeo.

Nordhaus, William D., "Do Real Output and Real Wage Measures Capture Reality? The History of Lighting Suggests Not," in Timothy F. Bresnahan and Robert J. Gordon, eds., The Economics of New Goods, University of Chicago Press, 1997, pp. 29–66.

Greenwood, Jeremy and Mehmet Yorukoglu, "1974," Carnegie Rochester Conference Series on Public Policy, 1997, 46, 49–95.

Klenow, Peter J., "Ideas vs. Rival Human Capital: Industry Evidence on Growth Models," Journal of Monetary Economics, August 1998, 42, 3–24.

Vintage Capital, Putty-Clay, Appropriate Technologies

Basu, Susanto and David N. Weil, "Appropriate Technology and Growth," Quarterly Journal of Economics, November 1998, 113 (4), 1025–1054.

Gilchrist, Simon and John C. Williams, "Putty Clay and Investment: A Business Cycle Analysis," Journal of Political Economy, October 2000, 108 (5), 928–960. and, "Transition Dynamics in Vintage Capital Models: Explaining the Post-war Experience of German and Japan," 2001. Boston University mimeo.

11. Growth over the Very Long Run

Diamond, Jared, Guns, Germs, and Steel, New York: W.W. Norton and Co., 1997.

Kremer, Michael, "Population Growth and Technological Change: One Million B.C. to 1990," Quarterly Journal of Economics, August 1993, 108 (4), 681–716.

Goodfriend, Marvin and John McDermott, "Early Development," American Economic Review, March 1995, 85 (1), 116–133.

Galor, Oded and David Weil, "Population, Technology, and Growth: From the Malthusian Regime to the Demographic Transition," American Economic Review, September 2000, 90, 806–828.

Hansen, Gary D. and Edward C. Prescott, "Malthus to Solow," 1998. NBER Working Paper No. 6858.

Lucas, Robert E., "The Industrial Revolution: Past and Future," 1998. University of Chicago mimeo.

Jones, Charles I., "Was an Industrial Revolution Inevitable? Economic Growth Over the Very Long Run," Advances in Macroeconomics, 2001, 1 (2), Article 1, ttp://www.bepress.com/bejm/advances/vol1/iss2/art1.

Clark, Gregory, "The Secret History of the Industrial Revolution," 2001. U.C. Davis mimeo.

12. R&D, Patents, and Productivity

Griliches, Zvi, ed., Chicago: University of Chicago Press, 1984., "Productivity Puzzles and R&D: Another Nonexplanation," Journal of Economic Perspectives, 1988, 2, 9–21., "Patents: Recent Trends and Puzzles," in Martin N. Baily and Clifford Winston, eds., Brookings Papers on Economic Activity, Microeconomics, Washington, D.C.: The Brookings Institution, 1989, pp. 291–330., "Productivity, R&D and the Data Constraint," American Economic Review, March 1994, 84 (1), 1–23.

Caballero, Ricardo J and Adam B. Jaffe, "How High are the Giants' Shoulders?" in Olivier Blanchard and Stanley Fischer, eds., NBER Macroeconomics Annual, Cambridge, MA: MIT Press, 1993, pp. 15–74.

Jones, Charles I. and John C. Williams, "Measuring the Social Return to R&D," Quarterly Journal of Economics, November 1998, 113, 1119–1135.

Kortum, Samuel, "Equilibrium R&D and the Patent-R&D Ratio: U.S. Evidence," American Economic Association Papers and Proceedings, May 1993, 83 (2), 450–457.

Kortum, Samuel S., "Research, Patenting, and Technological Change," Econometrica, 1997, 65 (6), 1389–1419.

Segerstrom, Paul, "Endogenous Growth Without Scale Effects," American Economic Review, December 1998, 88 (5), 1290–1310.

Kremer, Michael, "Patent Buyouts: A Mechanism for Encouraging Innovation," Quarterly Journal of Economics, November 1998, pp. 1137–1167.

13. Natural Resources, the Environment, and Growth

Jones, Charles I., Introduction to Economic Growth, New York: W.W. Norton and Co., 2002. Second Edition.

Nordhaus, William D., "Lethal Model 2: The Limits to Growth Revisited," Brookings Papers on Economic Activity, 1992, 2, 1–59.

Brander, James A. and M. Scott Taylor, "The Simple Economics of Easter Island: A Ricardo-Malthus Model of Renewable Resource Use," American Economic Review, March 1998, 88, 119–138.

Weitzman, Martin L., "Pricing the Limits to Growth from Minerals Depletion," Quarterly Journal of Economics, May 1999, 114 (2), 691–706.

14. Interesting and Accessible Readings

Diamond, Jared, Guns, Germs, and Steel, New York: W.W. Norton and Co., 1997.

DeLong, J. Bradford, "Slouching Toward Utopia," U.C. Berkeley (In progress). http://econ161.berkeley.edu/TCEH/Slouch_Old.html.

Easterly, William, The Elusive Quest for Growth: Economists' Adventures and Misadventures in the Tropics, MIT Press, 2001.

Solow, Robert M., Growth Theory: An Exposition, New York: Oxford University Press, 2000.

Simon, Julian L., The Ultimate Resource 2, Princeton, NJ: Princeton University Press,
1998

www.ingramcontent.com/pod-product-compliance
Lightning Source LLC
Chambersburg PA
CBHW052259220526
45471CB00001B/408